SIERRA NEVADA

Wildflowers

A FIELD GUIDE TO COMMON
WILDFLOWERS AND SHRUBS OF THE
SIERRA NEVADA, INCLUDING YOSEMITE, SEQUOIA,
AND KINGS CANYON NATIONAL PARKS

By Karen Wiese

FALCON®

HELENA, MONTANA

A **FALCON**GUIDE ®

Falcon® is continually expanding its list of recreational guidebooks. All books include detailed descriptions, accurate maps, and all the information necessary for enjoyable trips. You can order extra copies of this book and get information and prices for other Falcon® guidebooks by writing Falcon, P.O. Box 1718, Helena, MT 59624 or calling toll-free 1-800-582-2665. Please ask for a free copy of our current catalog. Visit our website at www.falcon.com or contact us by e-mail at falcon@falcon.com.

Project Editor: Tom Marino
Production Editor: Jessica Solberg
Copyeditor: Julie Schroeder
Map by Tony Moore
Illustrations by DD Dowden
Compositor: DD Dowden
Text design by Falcon Publishing, Inc.

Front cover photo of Arrow-leaved Balsamroot by Carol Grenier

Cataloging-in-Publication Data is on file at the Library of Congress.

CAUTION

All participants in the recreational activities suggested by this book must assume responsibility for their own actions and safety. The information contained in this guidebook cannot replace sound judgment and good decision-making skills, which help reduce risk exposure; nor does the scope of this book allow for disclosure of all the potential hazards and risks involved in such activities.

Learn as much as possible about the recreational activities in which you participate, prepare for the unexpected, and be cautious. The reward will be a safer and more enjoyable experience.

This book is dedicated to the loving memory
of my mother, Ruth Wiese,
who showed me the magic of flowers,
and my father, Robert Wiese,
who taught me the value of curiosity.

CONTENTS

# PREFACE

"I went out for a walk, and finally concluded to stay out till sundown,
for going out, I found, was really going in."
— JOHN MUIR, 1913

Long before my interest in flowers was ignited, I felt a profound sense of wonder as I hiked every trail, climbed each peak, and swam in every lake that I came to in the Sierra Nevada. With its infinite grace and profound beauty, my adventures there have always been extraordinary. On one level, the intent of this book is to satisfy a curiosity, to identify a plant; but on another level, the goal of this book is to inspire a sense of wonder about the life force. Elephant heads, fairy lanterns, and lady slippers—they are all here, and when you find them, there is an inexplicable sense of meeting with divinity. In her 1907 manual, *The Wild Flowers of California,* Mary Elizabeth Parsons describes this sense of wonder: "to the mind open to the great truths of the universe, it takes on a deeper significance. Such a mind sees in its often humble beginnings the genesis of things far-reaching and mighty. Two thousand years ago one grain of the showers of pollen wafted upon the wind and falling upon a minute undeveloped cone, quickened a seed there into life, and this dropping into the soil pushed up a tiny thread of green, which, after the quiet process of the ages, you now behold in the giant Sequoia which tosses its branches aloft, swept by the four winds of heaven."

This book will introduce you to 234 of the most common wildflowers, including shrubs, found in the Sierra Nevada. Because a book of this size cannot list each plant in the region, often an exact match will not be found. For example, more than fifty different lupines occur in the Sierra Nevada, making it impossible to include all members of the genus *Lupinus* in a book of this scope. Instead, several lupines were chosen that represent different colors, habitats, and plant communities with the hope that the reader will at least be able to identify the plant as a lupine and then use other resources to further identify the plant. The specific plants were chosen based on their distribution throughout the range, frequency of occurrence, and beauty.

My hope is that this book can serve to increase its readers' knowledge, appreciation, and awareness of the natural world.

ACKNOWLEDGMENTS

Contributions and encouragement to this book have come in many forms. I give heartfelt appreciation to all my friends and "my hikers" who have been supportive and enthusiastic about the book. I wish to express gratitude to colleagues who provided the first edits of portions of the rough draft: Michael Barbour, plant ecologist, University of California, Davis; Debra Bishop, president of the Sacramento Chapter, California Native Plant Society; Victoria Lake, botanist; Thomas Leatherman, Bureau of Land Management botanist; John Little, botanist; Elise Mattison, geologist; and Margriet Wetherwax, managing editor, Jepson Flora Project. Richard Hilton, geology professor at Sierra College, generously contributed the geology section of this book. Many of the concepts presented in this book required clarification and to these colleagues that assisted, I express my appreciation: Stephen J. Botti, National Park Service Fire Program planning manager; Joseph Meideros, biology professor at Sierra College; Kathleen Nelson, USDAFS forest botanist; Steve Schoenig, research scientist, California Department of Food and Agriculture; and Renee Shahrokh, botany professor at American River College. Many friends patiently accompanied me on my photographic forays and I am thankful for their company and their plant locating abilities: Cathy Anderson-Meyers, James Bailey, Jane Bicek, Mary Burns, Michael Fish, Tony Loftin, Sylvia Mehlhaff, Verlyn O'Neil, James Pompy, and Russel Towle.

I graciously thank Karen Callahan and Laurie Friedman, whose photographic assistance and friendship was so generously given. Richard Hanes was a valuable contributor of photographs. Julie Carville, Win and Bob Ehrhart, Carol Grenier, David Hennessy, Thomas Leatherman, Noel LaDue, Tony Loftin, Steve Matson, Dann McCright, and Joe Meideros generously volunteered photographs. Betsy Ringrose introduced me to her father, Edward J. Ringrose, M.D., through his photographs. Several of the late Dr. Ringrose's photographs appear in this book.

THE SIERRA NEVADA

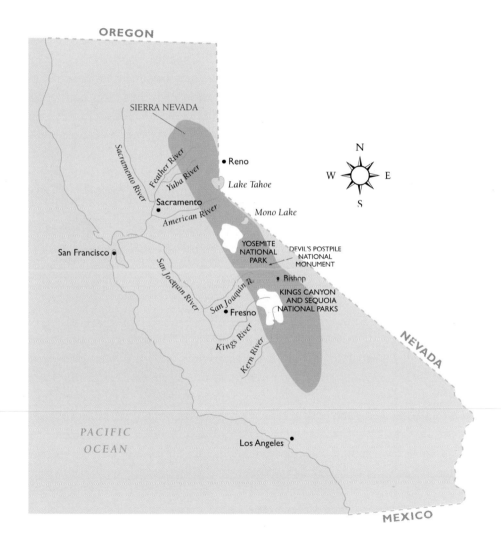

INTRODUCTION

The Sierra Nevada makes up one-fifth of California's total land mass and is California's largest mountain range, extending approximately 400 miles north to south and 50 to 80 miles west to east. Geologically, the Sierra Nevada extends from its northernmost point, several miles south of Lassen Peak, which is just south of the southernmost peak of the Cascade Range, to the Tehachapi Mountains at the Garlock Fault. However, the area covered by this book has as its northern border the North Fork of the Feather River in Plumas County; the southern border is the Greenhorn Mountains at Walker Pass, east of Bakersfield in Kern County. The western border of the Sierra Nevada abuts the foothills in a corridor of oak-dominated woodlands that transition westward into the Great Central Valley. The eastern border encompasses, at the northern boundary, the Sierra Valley and extends south through the east side of Lake Tahoe and follows State Route 395 south along the spectacular escarpment. It is the south part of the eastern border that rises so majestically with peaks that reach elevations of 14,000 feet. The area covered by this book contains Yosemite, Kings Canyon, and Sequoia National Parks as well as Lake Tahoe and Devils Postpile National Monument and the highest point in the contiguous United States, Mt. Whitney (14,494 feet).

Father Pedro Font, a Franciscan missionary in the Spanish expedition of Juan Bautista de Anza, which explored this area in 1776, viewed the mountains from a peak in San Francisco 180 miles away and called it *"una gran sierra nevada,"* which means a great snow-covered range. The naturalist John Muir, in his book *My First Summer in the Sierra,* wrote: "Probably more free sunshine falls on this majestic range than on any other in the world. . . . How ineffably spiritually fine is the morning-glow on the mountain-tops and the alpenglow of evening. Well may the Sierra be named, not the Snowy Range, but the Range of Light." The Sierra Nevada rises gradually from the west like a green wave, crests in snowcapped peaks, and plunges abruptly in a spectacular escarpment to the Owens Valley to the east.

The Sierra Nevada is a floristically diverse geographic region. The Sierra Nevada contains more than one half of California's 5,800 total species of flora! The area's unique combinations of topography and climate have presented the challenges that these plants, over time, have evolved to survive.

Geology

In the Jurassic Period, some 150 million years ago, the original Sierra Nevada was beginning to form as a high mountain range much like the Andes of South America today. This original Sierra Nevada formed as a large land mass, the North American Plate, drifted northwest and converged with the Pacific Plate. As the plates collided, the ancient sedimentary layers deposited on the ocean floor and the rocks of the Sierra were altered by intense heat and pressure. Some rock

Desolation Wilderness

CAROL GRENIER

materials deep under the mountain range melted and intruded into the core of the range as masses of hot liquid magma some miles in diameter. A portion of this material escaped as lava and ash through large volcanoes above, which periodically erupted copious amounts of volcanic debris. However, most of the molten rock slowly cooled and crystallized into the rock we know as granite and formed the backbone of the range. This granitic core is called the Sierra batholith and extends the entire length of the range.

About the time of the demise of the dinosaurs about 65 million years ago, this original Sierra Nevada was beginning to erode away and the granite below was being exposed for the first time. The ocean was beginning to lap on its western edge, depositing marine sediments, while a warm and humid climate favored tropical plants toward the interior. During this time erosion was the dominant force, and large ancestral rivers flowed from what is now central Nevada to their deltas at what is today the eastern edge of the Sacramento and

San Joaquin Valleys. The Sierra Nevada became a landscape looking more like the east coast mountains of North America than today's Sierra; it was a series of rolling hills and wide rivers flowing through a semitropical forest and stretched well into what is now Nevada.

About 30 million years ago, the climate began to get cooler, and renewed volcanism buried much of this landscape in white volcanic ash. There were numerous subsequent eruptions and lava and mudflows; by 10 million years ago, the Sierra was buried in lava debris. About this time, things began to change again as a slow uplift began to warp the western edge of this part of North America. About 5 million years ago this warp began to break at the present eastern edge of the Sierra and a renewed Sierra Nevada mountain range began to form. This great block of crust began to rise on its eastern edge and tilt toward the northwest. It began to resemble a three-ring binder laying closed on a table, with a long gentle slope on the west and a steep edge on the faulted eastern side. As the Sierra Nevada continued to uplift it left deep fault-bounded basins like Owens Valley and Carson Valley on its eastern edge.

As it grew higher, the Sierra gradually came to intercept most of the moisture carried by air currents from the west; it cut off the rains and then, increasingly, the snows, causing the arid Great Basin to form to the east. Rivers cut deep V-shaped canyons in both the eastern and western slopes of the Sierra, but as the climate cooled, snow in the higher elevations was converted to ice. This period, which lasted between about 2.5 million to 10,000 years ago, is known as the Ice Age. It was during this time that a series of warm-cold climate cycles caused much of the high country to be blanketed with an ice cap averaging 3,000 feet thick that was over 100 miles long and up to 40 miles wide. Glaciers carved the V-shaped valleys into U-shaped troughs and sculpted sharp ridges and peaks into the range. It was during this time that the spectacular landscape of Yosemite was formed and Muir's "Range of Light" was sculpted out of the white granitic core of the range. The glaciers created today's beautiful Sierran landscapes with deep valleys, cliffs, and ridges with magnificent peaks reflected in a myriad of glacially carved lakes. It was during this time that plants migrated up and down the Sierra with the shifts of the climate. The ice finally waned about 10,000 years ago, when today's climate was established. During the present period, the Sierra Nevada continues to uplift, and climatic trends are comparatively warm and temperate, characterized by warm summers and cold winters; it is in this short time span that the Sierra has been colonized by the present plant and animal species.

How to Use This Guide

The plant entries are divided into six color groups based on the most predominant color of the inflorescence. Please note that many flowers have more than one color and frequently a flower's color changes as it ages, so the reader is advised to refer to other color sections of the book. Within each color section, the plants are arranged alphabetically according to plant family. Each plant entry has a corresponding photograph. For the most part, images have been chosen that show identifying characteristics of the plant, including the flower, leaves, and habitat. Often, however, the photograph shows a close-up of the flower; in these cases, the reader is advised to read the description section to gain a sense of scale. The common names are based on those provided by *The Jepson Manual: Higher Plants of California* (Hickman, 1993) and *A California Flora and Supplement* (Munz and Keck, 1973). Although common names are not universally agreed upon, they are included here for the reader to gain an immediate sense of familiarity with the plant. Realize that, for example, the small, slender "sweet Cicely" of the Sierra Nevada is not the same three-foot tall plant of England with the same name. Scientific names, however, are recognized worldwide, and those included here are based on the nomenclature used in *The Jepson Manual.* The system we use today was created in the mid-eighteenth century by the Swedish naturalist Carolus Linnaeus. Scientific names are usually derived from a Latin word that describes a feature of the plant. Latin is used because it was the classical written language for medicine and law during the time of Linnaeus. Plants are placed into broad groupings called families, based on genetic, reproductive, chemical, and morphological similarities, which reflect a shared evolutionary history. An example of a family name is the pea family, the Fabaceae. Plants in this family include lupines, clovers, beans, and peas.

To identify each individual species, we employ a binomial system of classification, which assigns a two-word name to a plant. The first name is the genus name, which groups closely related plants based on similarities in flower and fruit. An example of a genus in the pea family is *Cercis*, which contains the redbud trees. The species name, which follows the genus name, groups plants that share a common ancestor and are isolated by reproduction or environment.

An example of a species name is *occidentalis,* which tells you that this redbud is the *western* redbud. Sometimes the name is further divided into subspecies or variety. Some of the wild plants that you observe will resemble plants that you already know. The Sierra Nevada pea may remind you of sweetpeas in your garden, which is no surprise, for they are in the same family.

The **Description** section of each entry contains information about the plant's life form and appearance, leaves, inflorescence, and often the fruit. The description section specifies the life form of the plant, indicating whether the plant is an annual, biennial, or perennial. Annual plants complete their life cycle in one year. Biennial plants grow vegetatively for one year, then produce seed and die the second year. Perennial plants live more than two growing seasons and are usually nonwoody above ground. Each plant is then described in terms of its physical appearance—whether the plant is an herb, a subshrub, shrub, tree, or vine. Herbs are broad-leaved, nonwoody plants that die back to the soil surface at the end of the growing cycle and can be annuals, perennials, or biennials. Subshrubs have woody lower stems; their nonwoody upper stems and twigs die back seasonally. Shrubs, on the other hand, have many woody branches and have a short maximum height. Subshrubs, shrubs, and trees are always perennials.

The leaves are described in terms of their arrangement on the stem as well as their shape. Leaves can be arranged opposite each other in pairs, or alternate on a stem, or whorled in a group of three or more on a stem, or arranged in a basal rosette. Leaves can also be simple or compound: A simple leaf has a single blade that may be lobed or cut, but not all the way to the midrib. A compound leaf has two or more blades call leaflets. Compound leaves may be arranged palmately or pinnately. (Figure 1.) Leaf margins can be entire, wavy, toothed (serrate), or lobed. (Figure 2.)

The inflorescence is the entire cluster of flowers and their associated structures, such as bracts in a paintbrush. The inflorescence can be arranged, for instance, in a spike, raceme, panicle, cyme, or umbel. (Figure 7.) An individual flower might be solitary at the end of a flower stalk or located in the leaf axil, and individual flowers might be shaped like a funnel, tube, bell, trumpet, sphere, saucer, or star. Members of the aster family (Asteraceae) are unique, for in this group, what appears to be one flower is actually a group of many flowers. The flower head is composed of either ray flowers, disk flowers, or both. On aster-family flowers with both flower types, such as daisies, the ray

Figure 1. Leaf Arrangement

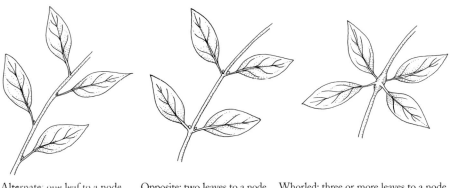

Alternate: one leaf to a node   Opposite: two leaves to a node   Whorled: three or more leaves to a node

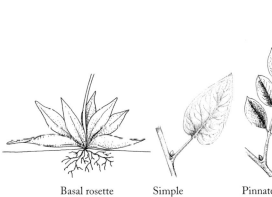

Basal rosette   Simple   Pinnately compound   Palmately compound
                                        leaves: leaflets   leaves: leaflets spreading
                                        arranged on both   like fingers from the
                                        sides of the petiole   palm of the hand

Figure 2. Leaf Margin

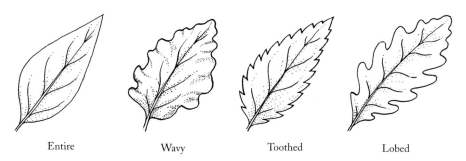

Entire   Wavy   Toothed   Lobed

Figure 3. Leaf Shape

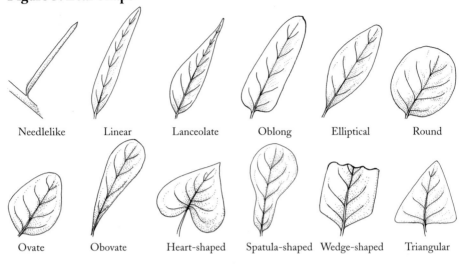

| Needlelike | Linear | Lanceolate | Oblong | Elliptical | Round |

| Ovate | Obovate | Heart-shaped | Spatula-shaped | Wedge-shaped | Triangular |

Figure 4. Typical Flower in Cross Section

Figure 5. Flower of the Pea Family (Fabaceae)

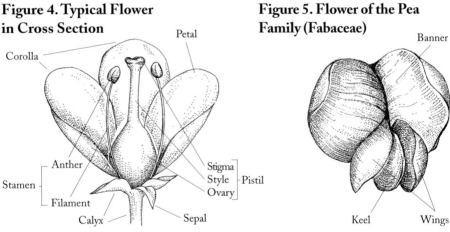

Figure 4 labels: Petal, Corolla, Anther, Stamen, Filament, Calyx, Sepal, Stigma, Style, Ovary, Pistil

Figure 5 labels: Banner, Keel, Wings

Figure 6. Flowers of the Sunflower Family (Asteraceae)

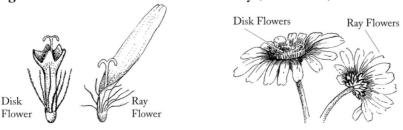

Disk Flower, Ray Flower, Disk Flowers, Ray Flowers

flowers resemble "petals," and the disk flowers form the "center." (Figure 6.)

Each flower has floral parts arranged in four concentric circles. The outer whorl consists of the sepals, collectively called the calyx, which are usually green but can be petal-like and colorful. Inside the ring of sepals are the petals, collectively called the corolla. The petals can be separate or fused. Fused petals can be partially fused, as in a monkeyflower, or entirely fused, as in a morning glory. Next, the stamens occur inside of the whorl of petals; there can be from zero to "many" stamens (the prickly poppy can have 250 stamens!). The stamens are the male reproductive structures; each stamen consists of a filament and anther; the anther produces the pollen. Then, in the center of the flower, one finds the pistil or pistils. Each pistil is generally subdivided into one or more stigmas, one or more styles, and an ovary. Inside the ovary are the ovules, which, when fertilized by a germinating pollen grain, produce seeds. (Figure 4.)

The fruit is the ripened ovary and associated structures. Some fruits are so unusual that they draw more attention than the flower; other times, all you will see is the fruit because the flower has already bloomed.

Many members of the pea family (Fabaceae) have a characteristic flower

Figure 7. Flower Arrangement or Inflorescence

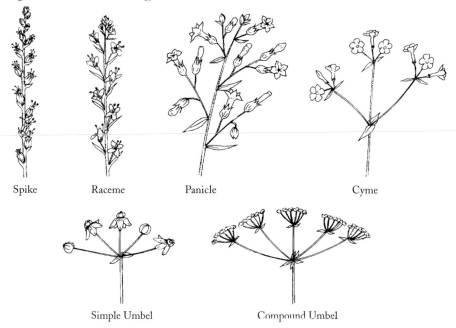

Spike   Raceme   Panicle   Cyme

Simple Umbel   Compound Umbel

shape. In this book, this arrangement will be referred to as a pea-family flower. The upper petal, called the banner, is erect, spreading, and usually the largest of the petals. Below this are two protruding side petals, called wings, which closely surround the bottom petal, the keel, which is created by the fusion of the two lowest petals. (Figure 5.)

The wildflower **bloom date** is based on information from several books, and months given represent the entire time the species may be found blooming anywhere in the Sierra. The blooming period for a plant varies with elevation, latitude, and local weather patterns. The same species will bloom earlier at lower elevations than the same species at higher elevation, and the same species will bloom earlier in the southern Sierra Nevada than the northern Sierra Nevada. Thus, you will have to allow for some variation in the bloom date for each individual location. If you miss a flower one month, you may be able to find that plant blooming at a higher elevation or farther north. Also note that plant bloom dates can vary by two to four weeks due to climatological variations; in years of heavy snows, wildflowers in the alpine zone may never bloom at all!

In general, the first flowers of spring begin blooming in the foothill woodlands of the southern Sierra Nevada in February. The same species will begin to bloom in March and April in the northern Sierra Nevada foothill woodlands. April and May are the peak blooming months for plants in the foothill woodlands. May, June, and July are peak blooming months for the mixed coniferous forest, and the sagebrush scrub on the east side. July and early August bring the spectacular displays of flowers in the mountain meadows and subalpine forest. In the high Sierra, spring is just beginning in late July, and the alpine zone becomes covered with a spectacular display of cushion plants. By early September most of the plants in the Sierra Nevada have bloomed, although some plants continue to bloom into October.

The specific environment in which a plant resides is termed its **habitat.** The four habitats covered in the scope of this book are (1) open places; (2) shaded areas in woodlands and forests; (3) wetlands including meadows (wet and dry), stream banks, lake edges, and seeps; and (4) rocky places including gravelly areas. In the alpine zone, gravelly and rocky areas are called alpine fellfields. Each habitat occurs as a result of the interactions of climate (temperature, precipitation, and humidity); soil (texture, moisture level, and chemical composition); and geography (location, elevation, and topography). To simplify the process of plant identification, the definitions of these habitat types are very broad in this manual. For example, an entry may state that the preferred habitat for a particular plant is "wetlands"; however, that plant may actually prefer drying meadows or moist stream banks—not what we would generally think of as a wetland. Additionally, many plants can live in more than one type of habitat; when this is the case, the most usual habitat for the plant is provided.

In this book, the **Habitat/Range** sections describe the plant community that the individual plant lives in. A plant community is a combination of living organisms and their interactions among themselves and with their environment. Plant communities are named for the dominant plant species; the five used in this book are taken from a synthesis of several resources. For more in-depth understanding, I call the reader's attention to the *Selected References* section of this book. For clarity and simplicity, the plant communities chosen in this book represent the vegetation of the Sierra Nevada on a gross scale and are based on dominant vegetation, soil, climate, and elevation. The careful observer will notice subdivisions within the broadly defined plant communities. The plant communities occur in north-south bands along fluctuating elevations of the Sierra Nevada. The bands are actually transitions of one plant community into another, much like a young adult transitions into middle age. One cannot detect exactly where the foothill woodland gives rise to the mixed coniferous forest. Plant communities are dynamic, changing in time because of plant succession, geologic and hydrologic forces, fire, and human influences. As you become more familiar with each plant community, you will be able to predict what plants may occur.

Foothill Woodland

The foothill woodland extends along the western side of the Sierra Nevada at an elevation of approximately 500 to 3,000 feet in the northern range of the Sierra Nevada, 800 to 4,000 feet in the central range, and 1,250 to 5,000 feet in the southern end of the range. The annual rainfall in this area is 15 to 40 inches, with most falling in the late fall, winter, and early spring. Average summer temperatures range from 75 to 96 degrees F, and average winter temperatures range from 29 to 42 degrees F; the growing season lasts 6 to 10

months. The foothill woodland is characterized by
foothill pine (*Pinus sabiniana*),
blue oak (*Quercus douglasii*),
interior live oak (*Quercus
wislizenii*), and California
buckeye (*Aesculus californica*),
and an understory of
ceanothus species and redbud
(*Cercis occidentalis*).

Mixed Coniferous Forest

The mixed coniferous forest,
referred to as the "Great
Green Wall" by author Elna
S. Bakker, extends along the
west side of the Sierra
Nevada at an elevation of
approximately 1,200 to 5,500
feet in the northern range of
the Sierra Nevada, 2,000 to
6,500 feet in the central
range, and 2,500 to 7,500 feet
in the southern end of the
range. This area receives
between 25 and 80 inches of
rainfall annually. Average
summer temperatures range
from 80 to 93 degrees F, and
average winter temperatures
range from 22 to 34 degrees
F; the growing season lasts 4

Foothill Woodland

Mixed Coniferous Forest

to 7 months. The mixed coniferous forest is characterized by large trees,
such as ponderosa pine (*Pinus ponderosa),* sugar pine (*Pinus lambertiana*),
Douglas-fir (*Pseudotsuga menziesii*), incense-cedar (*Calocedrus decurrens),*
white fir (*Abies concolor),* and black oak (*Quercus kelloggii*), and an understory

of manzanita (*Arctostaphylos* spp.), canyon live oak (*Quercus chrysolepis*), dogwood (*Cornus* spp.), and mountain misery (*Chamaebatia foliolosa*). Giant sequoias (*Sequoiadendron giganteum*) are found in pockets from the northernmost location in Placer County to the central and southern Sierra Nevada.

Subalpine Forest

The subalpine forest extends along both western and eastern slopes of the Sierra Nevada at an elevation of approximately 5,500 to 8,500 feet in the northern range of the Sierra Nevada, 6,500 to 10,000 feet in the central range, and 8,000 to 11,000 feet in the southern end of the range. The annual precipitation in this area is 35 to 65 inches, with most falling as snow. Average summer temperatures are below 85 degrees F, and average winter temperatures are well below 26 degrees F; the growing season lasts less than 4 months. The subalpine forest is characterized by California red fir (*Abies magnifica*), lodgepole pine (*Pinus contorta*), mountain hemlock (*Tsuga mertensiana*), and juniper (*Juniperus occidentalis*), and an understory of huckleberry oak (*Quercus vaccinifolia*) and red heather (*Phyllodoce breweri*). At the upper elevation of this range, near timberline, the vegetation transitions into sparsely forested whitebark pine (*Pinus albicaulis*), limber pine (*Pinus flexilis*), or foxtail pine (*Pinus balfouriana*).

Subalpine Forest

KAREN V/IESE

Alpine Zone

The alpine zone extends along both western and eastern slopes of the Sierra Nevada above timberline at elevations above approximately 8,500 feet in the northern range of the Sierra Nevada, above 10,000 feet in the central range, and above 10,500 feet in the southern end of the range. This area receives extreme wind, sunlight, and cold, with most precipitation evaporating in the wind. The growing season is measured in days and weeks, and plants living in the alpine zone have a correspondingly rapid blooming period. The alpine community is characterized by low-growing, cushionlike perennials. The rocky areas of the alpine community are called alpine fellfields. Some areas of the alpine zone, called nunataks,

Alpine Zone

KAREN WIESE

were never glaciated and contain an unusually high diversity of plants, many of which may have originated in the Great Basin and Rocky Mountains.

Pinyon-Juniper Woodland

The pinyon-juniper woodland forms pockets along the eastern side of the Sierra Nevada at an elevation of approximately 4,000 to 5,500 feet in the northern range and 5,000 to 8,000 feet in the southern end of the range. Pinyon-juniper woodland is often associated with

Pinyon-Juniper Woodland

KAREN WIESE

sagebrush, which forms an understory. Pinyon-juniper woodland requires 12 to 20 inches of precipitation per year, whereas sagebrush and its companion shrubs can survive on an average of seven inches per year. The pinyon-juniper woodland is characterized by pinyon pine (*Pinus monophylla*), juniper (*Juniperus* spp.), Jeffrey pine (*Pinus jeffreyi*), and an understory of sagebrush scrub (*Artemesia* spp.). Often, pinyon pine will occur in a pure stand or juniper without pinyon pine.

Sagebrush Scrub

The sagebrush scrub zone extends along the eastern side of the Sierra Nevada, locally in higher elevations on the west side in the Kings River Canyon, at an elevation of approximately 4,200 to 5,600 feet in the northern range, 6,000 to 7,000 feet in the southern end of the range, and into the Great Basin of Nevada. Average summer temperatures are in the 80s, and average winter temperatures range from 10 to 20 degrees F; the growing season lasts 2 to 5 months. Sagebrush scrub is characterized by low-growing shrubs such as sagebrush (*Artemisia* spp.), bitterbrush (*Purshia tridentata*), mountain mahogany (*Cercocarpus ledifolius*), and rabbitbrush (*Chrysothamnus* spp.), and may include open coniferous forests of pinyon pine (*Pinus monophylla*), Jeffrey pine (*Pinus jeffreyi*), lodgepole pine (*Pinus contorta* ssp. *murrayana*), and juniper (*Juniperus* spp.).

Sagebrush Scrub

The **Comments** sections include information that will help you become more acquainted with the significance of the name, history, edibility, and medicinal or Native American uses of each plant. This section provides the reader with a cursory introduction to some of the cultural uses of plants, but a number of books have been written about Native American uses of plants. The term Native American in this book generally applies to the Native American tribes in California, particularily those tribes that lived and still live in the region covered by this book. Some of these tribes are the Maidu, Washoe, Nisenan Miwok, Mono Paiute, Yokut, Monache, Owens Valley Paiute, and Tubatulabal. In fact, the Native American community is alive and thriving thoroughout the West. Although the majority of entries in this book list Native Americans as having "used" these plants, it is important to understand that most of these plants are currently being used by indigenous peoples.

As with all wild foods, a plant classified as "edible" should not necessarily be eaten. People have been poisoned, often fatally, by eating a misidentified plant; also, some people may have unique allergic reactions to plants, digestively or dermatologically. It is against the law to collect plants without written permission of the landowner, regardless of your intentions.

Before collecting any plant or plant part, dead or alive, on public lands, which include those administered by the USDA Forest Service, Bureau of Land Management, National Park Service, and National Monuments, you must have written permission from the appropriate institution. Resist the temptation to pick flowers, because when you pick a flower, you interrupt the plant's cycle of life, robbing it of its chance to reproduce.

As you use this manual, visiting different places in the Sierra Nevada, you will begin to discover your own special wildflower gardens. When you are just beginning, guided hikes, such as those offered by the California Native Plant Society (CNPS) will help you locate good wildflower viewing locations. The CNPS is a statewide organization of professionals and amateurs who have a common interest in learning about California's native flora and working to preserve it. A variety of educational programs and conservation efforts are sponsored by the CNPS, including field trips, plant sales, monthly meetings, and publications on native plants. The CNPS can be contacted at 1722 J Street, Suite 17, Sacramento, CA 95814; by calling (916) 447-2677; or by visiting their website at www.cnps.org. The *Selected References* section of this book lists books that describe wildflower viewing locations. If you are ready to venture out, any hiking trail in the Sierra Nevada will lead you to enchanting wildflower gardens. Enjoy!

BLUE AND PURPLE FLOWERS

KAREN WIESE

This section includes flowers ranging from pale blue to deep indigo and from lavender to violet. Since lavender flowers grade into pink, you should check the pink section if you do not find the flower you are looking for here.

Purple Milkweed

PURPLE MILKWEED
Asclepias cordifolia
Milkweed Family (Asclepiadaceae)

Description: Tall perennial with milky sap, up to 2' tall with opposite, clasping, ovate to heart-shaped leaves, 6" long. The inflorescence is an umbel of many unusual flowers. The 5 sepals are reflexed and the 5 petals are spreading, exposing a crown of 5 concave hoods. The long fruit encloses many tiny, tufted seeds.

May–July

Habitat/Range: Open or shaded, especially rocky places in foothill woodland and mixed coniferous forest.

Comments: The genus name honors the Greek physician Asklepios. The species name is Latin for "heart-leaved." This plant yields a fiber that Native Americans used for rope. The plant itself was used as a contraceptive and snakebite remedy. The larvae of the monarch butterfly (*Danaus plexippus*) feed on the leaves of milkweeds.

ALPINE ASTER
Aster alpigenus var. *andersonii*
Aster Family (Asteraceae)

Description: Spreading to erect perennial, 3–16" long. The leaves are linear, occur mostly at the base of the plant, and are up to 10" long. There is only 1 saucer-shaped flower head per stem. The flower heads, which can be up to 1" wide, have purple ray flowers surrounding yellow disk flowers.

June–September

Habitat/Range: Wetlands, especially meadows, in mixed coniferous forest, subalpine forest, and the alpine zone.

Comments: The genus name is Greek for "star," referring to the shape of the disk-flower corollas. The species name is Latin for "alpine," which is where this plant is predominantly found.

Alpine Aster

WANDERING DAISY
Erigeron peregrinus
Aster Family (Asteraceae)

Description: Perennial 3–18" tall, branched above, and often grows in large colonies. The oblanceolate leaves are 2–8" long and are primarily basal. The leaves along the stem become somewhat reduced upward and are lanceolate to ovate in shape. The inflorescence is a flat-topped cluster of 1–4 flower heads with purple ray flowers and yellow disk flowers. The flower heads are up to 1" in diameter.

July–September

Habitat/Range: Open areas, wetlands, and rocky places in mixed coniferous forest, subalpine forest, and the alpine zone.

Comments: The genus name is Greek for "early old age," referring to the ancient name of an early flowering plant covered with white hairs. The species name is Latin for "exotic" or "foreign."

Wandering Daisy

Hoary-Aster

HOARY-ASTER
Machaeranthera canescens
Aster Family (Asteraceae)

Description: Glandular, annual to short-lived perennial, up to 2' tall, with loosely spreading branches. The linear leaves are 1–4" long with serrate margins. The inflorescence is a cluster of flower heads with purple ray flowers and yellow disk flowers. The base of the flower head is narrow.

July–October

Habitat/Range: Open areas in mixed coniferous forest, pinyon-juniper woodland, and sagebrush scrub.

Comments: The genus name is Greek for "swordlike anthers." The species name means "grayish," referring to the slightly grayish cast to the stem and leaves.

Large Hound's Tongue

LARGE HOUND'S TONGUE
Cynoglossum grande
Borage Family (Boraginaceae)

Description: Perennial with one generally leafless stem, 3' tall. The leaves are ¾" long, ovate, with a hairy lower surface and smooth upper surface. The inflorescence is a cluster of small, trumpet-shaped flowers, less than ¾" wide. Each 5-lobed flower has small, white appendages in the center of the flower. The round fruits have short spines.

March–June

Habitat/Range: Shaded areas in foothill woodland and mixed coniferous forest.

Comments: The genus name of this plant is Greek for "dog's tongue." It was thought that a good hunting dog should have a bluish tongue like the color of the flowers. Others contend that the shape of the leaves resemble a dog's tongue. Some Native Americans make a poultice from the roots to relieve pain and swelling.

STICKSEED
Hackelia velutina
Borage Family (Boraginaceae)

Description: Hairy perennial up to 12–30" tall. The leaves are elliptic to oblanceolate, hairy, and 2–9" long. The inflorescence is an open panicle of tubular flowers that are ¾" long. The fruits are ¼" long with many prickles.

June–August

Habitat/Range: Open, especially dry areas in mixed coniferous forest and subalpine forest.

Comments: The genus name honors the Czech botanist Joseph Hackel (1783–1869). The species name is Latin for "velvety," referring to the soft hairs covering this plant. The name "stickseed" comes from the prickles on the fruits, which get transported by sticking to animal fur as well as the clothing of humans.

Stickseed

Streamside Bluebells; Languid Ladies

STREAMSIDE BLUEBELLS; LANGUID LADIES

Mertensia ciliata
Borage Family (Boraginaceae)

Description: Perennial with many leafy stems, 1–5' tall. The leaves are alternate, lanceolate, and 2–5" long. The inflorescence is an open panicle of nodding, tubular flowers, each less than ¾" long. The corolla may be blue or pink.

May–August

Habitat/Range: Wetlands in mixed coniferous forest and subalpine forest.

Comments: The genus name honors the German botanist Franz K. Mertens (1764–1831). The species name is Latin for "hairy edges," referring to the tiny hairs on the leaves. Plants in this genus are often called "lungworts," referring to a European plant whose spotted leaves suggested a diseased lung and therefore a curative agent for lung ailments.

KAREN WIESE

Mountain Jewelflower

MOUNTAIN JEWELFLOWER
Streptanthus tortuosus
Mustard Family (Brassicaceae)

Description: Annual to subshrub up to 3' tall. The leaves are 1–3" long and clasp the stem, giving the appearance of a shield, yielding an alternate common name, shieldleaf. As the leaves age, they turn yellow. The ½" flower has a purple, urn-shaped calyx and 4 purple or yellow, linear, reflexed petals. The fruit is up to 4 ¾" long.

April–September

Habitat/Range: Open areas and rocky places in foothill woodland, mixed coniferous forest, and subalpine forest.

Comments: The genus name is Greek for "twisted flower," referring to the wavy-leaved petals. The species name is Latin for "much twisted," again referring to the flowers.

CALIFORNIA HAREBELL
Campanula prenanthoides
Bellflower Family (Campanulaceae)

Description: Reclining or erect perennial up to 30" tall. The leaves are lanceolate to ovate and are up to 2 ½" long, with serrate margins. The nodding, bell-shaped flowers are in clusters of 2–5 each. The flowers have 5 curved petals, are ½" long, and have an exserted style.

June–September

Habitat/Range: Open areas in mixed coniferous forest and often in redwood forests.

Comments: The genus name is Latin for "little bell," referring to the shape of the corolla.

KAREN CALLAHAN

California Harebell

BACIGALUPI'S DOWNINGIA
Downingia bacigalupii
Bellflower Family (Campanulaceae)

Description: Annual up to 16" tall. The leaves are small and lanceolate and are often gone before flowering. The inflorescence is a spike of 5-lobed tubular flowers, each up to ¾" wide. The 2 upper petals are pointed and are smaller than the 3 fused, rounded lower petals. The lower petals have 2 oblong, orange-yellow spots in a central white field.

May–July

Habitat/Range: Wetlands in mixed coniferous forest and sagebrush scrub.

Comments: The genus name honors the first great American landscape gardener and horticulturalist, Andrew Jackson Downing (1815–1852). The species name honors California botanist Rimo Charles Bacigalupi (1901–1996), the first curator of the Jepson Herbarium at the University of California, Berkeley.

Bacigalupi's Downingia

SIERRA NEVADA PEA
Lathyrus nevadensis var. *nevadensis*
Pea Family (Fabaceae)

Description: Perennial, 6–14" tall, with tendrils. The leaves are compound and have 4–8 elliptic, paired leaflets. The inflorescence is a cluster of 2–4 pea-family flowers. The flowers are up to 1" long with a white keel and a purple banner that is reflexed.

April–June

Habitat/Range: Shaded and dry areas in mixed coniferous forest.

Comments: The genus name is the ancient Greek name of an unidentified plant in the pea family. The larvae of the western tailed-blue butterfly (*Everes amyntula*) feed on the leaves. This plant is toxic to humans and livestock.

Sierra Nevada Pea

Brewer's Lupine

KAREN CALLAHAN

BREWER'S LUPINE
Lupinus breweri
Pea Family (Fabaceae)

Description: Hairy perennial or subshrub that appears as a silvery mat growing to 8" tall from a woody base. The palmately compound leaves have 5–10 leaflets up to ¾" long clustered at the base of the plant. The inflorescence is a spike of blue pea-family flowers. Each flower is almost ½" long with a white or yellow patch on the banner. The fruit is silky, ¾" long with 3–4 seeds.

June–August

Habitat/Range: Open places in mixed coniferous forest, subalpine forest, and the alpine zone.

Comments: This plant is adapted to the harsh subalpine and alpine environments. The low stature of the plant protects it from high winds. The silver hairs reflect the harmful intense light of high elevations. The hairs also create a "boundary layer" or protective layer of trapped air that prevents desiccation from the wind.

SIERRA GENTIAN
Gentianopsis holopetala
Gentian Family (Gentianaceae)

Description: Annual or perennial, erect or sprawling, up to 20" tall, with the stem often branched. The leaves are opposite and range from linear upper leaves that are ¾" long to spoon-shaped lower leaves that are 1 ½" long. The flowers are funnel shaped, 4-lobed, 1–2" long, occur 1 per stem, and have a dark rib on the calyx.

July–September

Habitat/Range: Wetlands, especially meadows, in mixed coniferous forest, subalpine forest, and the alpine zone.

Comments: The genus name is Greek for "resembling *Gentiana*," referring to another similar genus. Gentian flowers close at night and during cloudy weather, conserving pollen for the pollinators, which are most active during fair-weather days.

Sierra Gentian

KAREN WIESE

Large-Leaf Lupine

LARGE-LEAF LUPINE
Lupinus polyphyllus
Pea Family (Fabaceae)

Description: Perennial up to 5' tall. The leaves are palmately compound, with 5–17 leaflets. The inflorescence is a 2–16" spike of many flowers along the flower stalk. Each pea-family flower has a yellow to white patch on the banner. The hairy fruit is beanlike, up to 1 ½" long.

May–August

Habitat/Range: Wetlands in mixed coniferous forest and subalpine forest.

Comments: The genus name is derived from the Latin word for "wolf," lupus. When lupines were first named, it was from the mistaken idea that the plants rob the soil of nutrients, since they were always found in disturbed areas. The lupines inspired the comparison to a pack of wolves destroying a barnyard of animals. However, the opposite is actually true. Lupines and other members of the pea family have bacteria in nodules on their roots. These bacteria actually convert atmospheric nitrogen into a form that the plants can utilize. In turn, the bacteria gain food and are protected in the nodule. Lupines have alkaloids concentrated in the seeds that are toxic to humans, cattle, and sheep. The plants, however, provide food for wildlife. The larvae of the arrowhead blue butterfly (Glaucopsyche piasus) feed on the leaves.

DAN MCCRIGHT

Star Swertia Felwort

STAR SWERTIA FELWORT
Swertia perennis
Gentian Family (Gentianaceae)

Description: Perennial up to 18" tall. At the base, the leaves are spoon shaped to obovate, and along the stem, the leaves are elliptical. The 5-petaled, star-shaped flowers are almost 1" wide. The petals have dark purple veins, and 2 fringed nectary glands appear at the base of each petal. The corolla can also be greenish white.

July–September

Habitat/Range: Wetlands, especially meadows, in subalpine forest and the alpine zone.

Comments: The species name means "perennial."

KAREN CALLAHAN / RICHARD HANES

Sierra Gooseberry

SIERRA GOOSEBERRY
Ribes roezlii
Gooseberry Family (Grossulariaceae)

Description: Spiny-stemmed shrub up to 3' tall. The leaves are serrate and round, up to 1" wide, and paler on the undersides. The inflorescence is a raceme of 1–3 nodding flowers. Each flower has 5 purple, reflexed sepals and 5 white petals with inward curving margins and 5 exserted red stamens. The fruit is a red berry with stout prickles.

May–July

Habitat/Range: Open areas in mixed coniferous forest and subalpine forest.

Comments: The genus name is the ancient Arabic name for plants of this genus. The berries are edible raw, cooked, or dried.

WOOLEN-BREECHES
Hydrophyllum capitatum var. *alpinum*
Waterleaf Family (Hydrophyllaceae)

Description: Short, hairy perennial up to 10"
tall. The leaves are pinnately compound, with
7–15 deeply lobed leaflets. The inflorescence
is a sphere of many bell-shaped purple flowers, often hidden at the base of the plant, under the leaves. The petals are slightly lobed at
the outer edges. The stamens and style are exserted. The flowers can be purple to white with
lavender markings.

May–June

Habitat/Range: Wetlands in mixed coniferous forest and sagebrush scrub.

Comments: The genus name is Greek for "water leaf," referring to the way the plant cradles
water droplets on the leaves. The species name
is Latin for "headlike," referring to the inflorescence. This plant was an important early
spring food for many Native Americans.

Woolen-Breeches

BABY BLUE-EYES
Nemophila menziesii
Waterleaf Family (Hydrophyllaceae)

Description: Annual, sprawling plant up to 1'
long. The leaves are ½–3" long, lobed, and are
arranged opposite each other on the stem. The
bright blue saucer-shaped corolla is ½–1" wide
with a white center and often has black speckles.

March–June

Habitat/Range: Open areas, especially meadows, in foothill woodland and mixed coniferous forest.

Comments: The genus name is Greek for
"grove-loving," referring to the woodland habitat of many species in this genus. The species
name honors Archibald Menzies (1754–1842),
a Scottish naturalist and surgeon who explored
the Pacific Coast in 1792. The explorer John
C. Fremont (1813–1890) wrote that "the blue
fields of nemophila and the golden poppy represent fairly the skies and gold of California."

Baby Blue-Eyes

Western Blue Flag

WESTERN BLUE FLAG
Iris missouriensis
Iris Family (Iridaceae)

Description: Perennial, up to 2' tall, from a rhizome that is up to 1" in diameter. The leaves are lanceolate, up to 18" long, and often have a purplish base. The inflorescence has 1–2 blue flowers, 4–5" across. The 3 petal-like sepals turn downward, acting as a landing pad for insects. The sepals also have purple veins or nectar guides to attract insects to the nectar. Each sepal has a stamen just beneath a petal like style. The 3 petals are erect. When an insect lands on a sepal, it crawls into the center of the plant toward the nectar, brushing up against the style and thus rubbing another flower's pollen onto it as it picks up a new load of pollen.

May–July

Habitat/Range: Wetlands in mixed coniferous forest and subalpine forest, mostly on the east side of the Sierra Nevada.

Comments: The genus name is Greek for "rainbow," referring to the many flower colors. It is also the name of the classical Greek messenger of the Olympian Gods and emissary of the Great Mother, Hera, who revealed her presence as a rainbow. Iris was an important plant for some Native Americans. The leaves are woven into mats and lined with cattail "down" for baby diapers.

BLUE-EYED GRASS
Sisyrinchium bellum
Iris Family (Iridaceae)

Description: Perennial, often multistemmed, up to 25" tall, from a rhizome, with narrow and grasslike leaves. The blue-purple flowers are trumpet shaped, ½" wide, and have 3 petal-like sepals and 3 petals. The sepals and petals have purple nectar guides and the throat of the flower is bright yellow.

July–August

Habitat/Range: Wetlands in foothill woodland and mixed coniferous forest.

Comments: The genus name is the ancient Greek name of an irislike plant. Some Native Americans used the roots to make a tea that was used as a laxative. The species name is Latin for "beautiful" or "handsome."

KAREN WIESE

Blue-Eyed Grass

RICHARD HANES

Mountain Monardella; Pennyroyal

MOUNTAIN MONARDELLA; PENNYROYAL
Monardella odoratissima
Mint Family (Lamiaceae)

Description: Aromatic perennial with a 4-sided stem, 6–14" tall. The leaves are entire, up to 2" long, lanceolate, and often hairy. The inflorescence is a 1" wide sphere of many flowers with leaflike bracts at the base. Each flower is ¾" long and asymmetrical, with a 2-lipped corolla. The upper lip has 2 lobes fused together and held erect, and the bottom lip has 3 lobes fused and recurved. The 4 stamens are exserted from the corolla in two pairs of unequal length.

June–September

Habitat/Range: Shaded areas in mixed coniferous forest and sagebrush scrub.

Comments: The genus name honors the Spanish botanist and physician Nicolas Monardes (1493–1588). The common name, pennyroyal, is actually a corruption of the French *pulial royal*, a royal flea remedy.

Selfheal

SELFHEAL
Prunella vulgaris var. *lanceolata*
Mint Family (Lamiaceae)

Description: Often hairy, sprawling to erect perennial, up to 20" long. The leaves are ovate, 1–3" long, and opposite on a 4-sided stem. The inflorescence is a spike of densely clustered flowers. The flowers are tubular and have a calyx that almost hides the 1–1 ½" corolla. The asymmetrical corolla is 2-lipped, with the upper and lower lips the same length. The upper lip is hoodlike over the reproductive parts. The lower lip has a broad middle petal that acts as a landing pad for pollinating insects.

May–September

Habitat/Range: Wetlands and shaded areas in mixed coniferous forest, especially meadows.

Comments: The genus name is from an early German name for a plant used to treat chest pains, sore throats, and a wide variety of ailments—wounds treated with a poultice of this plant would "self-heal." The species name is Latin for "common," referring to the wide range of habitats that this plant can survive.

KAREN CALLAHAN

Harvest Brodiaea

HARVEST BRODIAEA
Brodiaea elegans
Lily Family (Liliaceae)

Description: Perennial from a corm, up to 2' tall. The 3–5 linear leaves occur at the base of the plant and are 4–16" long; these die back before the flower blooms. The inflorescence is an umbel of many funnel-shaped flowers. Each flower has 3 petal-like sepals and 3 petals, 1–1 ½" long. Inside the flower are 3 stamens and 3 staminodes (sterile stamens).

April–July

Habitat/Range: Open areas in foothill woodland and mixed coniferous forest.

Comments: The genus name honors the Scottish botanist J. J. Brodie (1759–1828). The species name is Latin for "elegant." The corms of this plant were an important staple food of the Native Americans.

WILD HYACINTH
Dichelostemma multiflora
Lily Family (Liliaceae)

Description: Perennial rising up to 2' from a corm. The 3–4 leaves are linear and 1–3' long at the base of the plant. The 2" wide inflorescence is an umbel of 10–35 purple-pink flowers. Each bell-shaped flower has 3 petal-like sepals and 3 petals and a tightly constricted neck, just above the ovary. Each flower is up to 1" long. The filaments are fused into the petals.

April–June

Habitat/Range: Open areas in foothill woodland and mixed coniferous forest.

Comments: The genus name is Greek for "toothed crown," referring to the filaments that are fused to the petals in a crownlike tube. The species name is Latin for "many flowered," referring to the many flowers in the inflorescence.

KAREN WIESE

Wild Hyacinth

Camas Lily

CAMAS LILY
Camassia quamash
Lily Family (Liliaceae)

Description: Perennial rising up to 4' from a bulb, and grows in masses in wet places. The leaves are linear and 6–24" long. The inflorescence is a raceme of at least 3 deep purple flowers. The star-shaped flowers are 1–2" wide and have 3 petal-like sepals and 3 petals. The anthers are bright yellow with a single green style.

May–June

Habitat/Range: Wetlands in mixed coniferous forest and subalpine forest.

Comments: The genus name is derived from the Nez Perce Indian name for this plant, which means "sweet." The bulbs were a major food source for Native Americans who lived near these bulbs. The preparation of the camas bulbs was a community festival. The bulbs were slow-roasted for 24–36 hours on branches of alder or birch in pits of warm ashes. After the bulbs were removed from the fire pit and cooled, the women would peel and press the bulbs between their hands, forming them into "cookies" that taste somewhat like brown sugar.

KAREN CALLAHAN

Trillium

TRILLIUM
Trillium angustipetalum
Lily Family (Liliaceae)

Description: Perennial with a musty odor, 6–27" tall. Each plant has 3 oval leaves that are arranged in a whorl. The flower is up to 4" long and has 3 green sepals and 3 purple petals.

March–June

Habitat/Range: Shaded areas in foothill woodland and mixed coniferous forest.

Comments: The genus name is Latin for "three," referring to the leaves. Some Native Americans used the root of this plant to make a tonic to help stop nosebleeds and the bleeding of menstruation and childbirth. Another common name for this plant is wake-robin, referring to the arrival of robins and trilliums early in the spring.

WESTERN BLUE FLAX
Linum lewisii
Flax Family (Linaceae)

Description: Slender perennial up to 30" tall. The leaves are linear, ¼–1" long, and alternate. The inflorescence is a raceme of several 5-petaled blue flowers, ¾–1 ½" wide, nodding in bud. The fruit contains 10 shiny brown seeds.

May–September

Habitat/Range: Open areas in mixed coniferous forest, subalpine forest, pinyon-juniper woodland, sagebrush scrub, and the alpine zone.

Comments: The genus name is Latin for "flax." The species name honors Meriwether Lewis (1774–1809). Some Native Americans soaked the root for an eye medicine, and the stem to make a medicine for upset stomachs. Native Americans also eat the roasted and ground seeds, and use the stems for cordage.

CAROL GRENIER

Western Blue Flax

NAKED BROOMRAPE
Orobanche uniflora
Broomrape Family (Orobanchaceae)

Description: Hairy, glandular plant with no true leaves, up to 2" tall. The tubular flower, ½–1 ½" long, is slightly curved. The lavender, 5-lobed corolla is 2 lipped, with 2 lobes on the top and 3 on the bottom. This plant is root parasitic on herbaceous plants such as *Sedum* and plants in the families Asteraceae and Saxifragaceae.

May–August

Habitat/Range: Wetlands in mixed coniferous forest and subalpine forest.

Comments: The genus name is the Greek name of a plant that is parasitic on vetch. The species name is Latin for "one flowered," referring to the solitary flower per plant. The common name, broomrape, refers to the tuberous growth (*rapum* is Latin for "turnip") caused by this plant's parasitism on the roots of broom plants.

Naked Broomrape

JACOB'S LADDER
Polemonium californicum
Phlox Family (Polemoniaceae)

Description: Perennial with soft hairs, 1' tall. The leaves are pinnately compound and have approximately 12 pairs of lanceolate leaflets. The inflorescence is a loose cluster of blue-purple bell-shaped flowers, each ½" wide, with a white tube and blue or yellow throat. The 3-parted style and stamens are exserted from the flower.

June–August

Habitat/Range: Open and shaded areas in mixed coniferous forest and subalpine forest.

Comments: The genus name is thought to honor Polemon, an early Greek philosopher. The common name, Jacob's ladder, based on the arrangement of the leaflets, comes from the story in Genesis 28:12 of Jacob's dream of a ladder connecting heaven and earth.

Jacob's Ladder

Sky Pilot

SKY PILOT
Polemonium eximium
Phlox Family (Polemoniaceae)

Description: Dense, hairy perennial up to 15" tall. The leaves are glandular, compound, 1–4" long, linear in outline, and have many finely lobed leaflets. The inflorescence is a sphere, 1 ½" wide, of many fragrant, blue to purple, funnel-shaped flowers, each ½" long. Each corolla has 5 blue lobes and a white corolla tube.

July–August

Habitat/Range: Rocky places in the upper elevations of the alpine zone.

Comments: The species name is Latin for "distinguished; out of the ordinary." Sky pilot grows at the highest elevation of any plant in the Sierra Nevada! The common name is a nickname for a person who leads others to heaven, because this plant grows only on lofty peaks.

MONKSHOOD
Aconitum columbianum
Buttercup Family (Ranunculaceae)

Description: Perennial up to 6' tall. The palmately lobed leaves are 1–7" long with 3–5 deep lobes and serrate leaf edges. The inflorescence is a raceme of oddly shaped deep purple flowers. The sepals are petal-like. The uppermost of the 5 sepals is shaped like a hood, hence the common name. The side sepals are round and the lower sepals are linear; both enclose the small petals. The 2 true petals are hidden inside the "hood."

July–August

Habitat/Range: Wetlands in mixed coniferous forest and subalpine forest.

Comments: The genus name is the ancient Greek name of this plant. This plant is very toxic, causing deaths in humans and livestock. An alternate common name, wolfsbane, comes from the medieval practice of using the juice to poison arrows used to hunt wolves.

KAREN WIESE / EDWARD

Monkshood

KAREN WIESE

Slender Larkspur

SLENDER LARKSPUR
Delphinium gracilentum
Buttercup Family (Ranunculaceae)

Description: Perennial up to 20" tall. The leaves are palmately lobed and occur on the lower third of the stem. The inflorescence is a raceme of as many as 15–20 purple flowers along the stem. The flowers are 1" long, have 5 petal-like sepals, and 4 tiny petals inside. The bottom sepal is deeply notched. The upper sepal is reflexed to form a spur 1" long. The sepals can be blue, white, or pink.

May–July

Habitat/Range: Shaded, often moist areas in foothill woodland and mixed coniferous forest.

Comments: The common name refers to the large spur on a lark's back toe, which resembles the spur on the flower. The genus name is from the Latin *delphinus*, "dolphin," referring to the shape of the flower bud. The species name means "slender," referring to the thin stem. All delphiniums are poisonous to humans and livestock.

RICHARD HANES

Mahala Mat

MAHALA MAT
Ceanothus prostratus
Buckthorn Family (Rhamnaceae)

Description: Prostrate shrub, up to 8' wide. The leaves are opposite, 1" long, and evergreen. The inflorescence is an umbel of deep blue, lavender, or purple saucer-shaped flowers. The flowers have petal-like sepals and 5 spoon-shaped petals. The fruit is round, 3-chambered, and filled with 3 seeds.

April–June

Habitat/Range: Open areas in foothill woodland and mixed coniferous forest.

Comments: The genus name is Greek for "thorny plant," referring to the thorns on several species. The species name is Latin for "prostrate," referring to its growth form. Some Native Americans used the flowers as a soap, rubbing them together with water. The branches were hardened in fire and used as digging sticks to unearth edible plant parts such as bulbs and rhizomes.

California Pitcher Plant; Cobra Lily

CALIFORNIA PITCHER PLANT; COBRA LILY
Darlingtonia californica
Pitcher-Plant Family (Sarraceniaceae)

Description: An uncommon insectivorous perennial that can be 4–36" tall. The tubular leaf has evolved to capture flying insects; the hood has translucent areas that suggest an escape route, but inside the leaf there are slippery surfaces and stiff reflexed hairs that make escape impossible. The moisture in the base of the leaves contains enzymes that digest the insects, thereby making the nutrients available to the plant. The leaf has 2 yellow to purple-green appendages at the top. The flowers are nodding, 1–2" wide, and have 5 yellow-green oblong sepals that surround 5 purple petals.

April–June

Habitat/Range: Wetlands, especially nutrient deficient seeps on serpentine, in mixed coniferous forest in the northeastern Sierra Nevada (Plumas and Nevada Counties).

Comments: The genus name honors the American botanist William Darlington (1782–1863). This plant is endemic to serpentine substrates; trapping and devouring insects helps it to compensate for nutrient deficiencies in the serpentine soils.

RICHARD HANES

Blue-Eyed Mary

BLUE-EYED MARY
Collinsia torreyi
Figwort Family (Scrophulariaceae)

Description: Annual up to 10" tall that often carpets slopes. The leaves are opposite, linear to ovate, and ¾–1 ½" long. The flowers are ½" long and 2-lipped with 5 lobes. The upper 2 lobes are reflexed, whitish, and often blue tipped. The lower 3 lobes, which look like 2 petals, are violet-blue and longer than the upper ones. The center of the 3 bottom lobes is keeled and difficult to see.

April–July

Habitat/Range: Open areas, often in sandy soils, in mixed coniferous forest and subalpine forest.

Comments: The genus honors the Philadelphia botanist Zaccheus Collins (1764–1831). The species name honors the American botanist and chemistry professor John Torrey (1796–1873). The white upper lip draws insects to the nectar and the contrasting lower lip of this plant offers a good landing spot.

KAREN WIESE

Timberline Penstemon

TIMBERLINE PENSTEMON
Penstemon davidsonii var. *davidsonii*
Figwort Family (Scrophulariaceae)

Description: Mat-forming and woody sub-shrub up to 4" tall. The leaves are elliptic, evergreen, 1" long, and opposite. The flowers occur in pairs in the axils of the upper leaves. The flowers are 2-lipped, trumpet shaped, and up to 1 ½" long; the top lip is 2-lobed, and the bottom lip is 3-lobed. The flowers are large relative to the plant, which helps to attract pollinators at this high elevation. The floor of the corolla's throat is covered with white hairs that function to brush pollen off of pollinators. The flower has 4 stamens and 1 staminode, which is a sterile stamen half the length of the stamens.

July–August

Habitat/Range: Rocky places in subalpine forest and the alpine zone.

Comments: The genus name is both Latin and Greek for "almost thread," referring to the thin, stamenlike staminode. The species name honors Professor George Davidson (1825–1911), a geographer and astronomer who collected this plant in Yosemite in 1890s.

KAREN CALLAHAN

Foothill Penstemon

FOOTHILL PENSTEMON
Penstemon heterophyllus
Figwort Family (Scrophulariaceae)

Description: Perennial up to 5' tall. The leaves are opposite, linear to oblanceolate, and tapered at the base. The flowers occur in pairs in the axils of the leaves. Each flower is trumpet shaped with 2 lips, blue, and 1–1 ½" long with a white throat.

April–July

Habitat/Range: Open areas in foothill woodland and mixed coniferous forest.

Comments: The genus *Penstemon* is the largest genus of flowering plants endemic to North America. Most of its 250 species occur in the western United States.

MEADOW PENSTEMON; WHORLED PENSTEMON
Penstemon rydbergii var. *oreocharis*
Figwort Family (Scrophulariaceae)

Description: Perennial, 6–24" tall, often growing in masses. The leaves are opposite, lanceolate, and 1–3" long. The inflorescence is a whorl of 1–6 distinct clusters of purple flowers. Each trumpet-shaped flower has 5 petals fused into a 2-lipped tube, ⅜–½" long. The throat floor is covered with white hairs, with a bright yellow, hairy staminode inside the flower that entices insects to enter to gather nectar and pollinate the flowers.

May–August

Habitat/Range: Wetlands in mixed coniferous forest, subalpine forest, and sagebrush scrub.

Comments: The species name honors Axel Rydberg (1860–1931), an engineer who was also curator of the New York Botanical Garden and who wrote several floras. The variety name is Latin for "mountain beauty."

KAREN WIESE

Meadow Penstemon; Whorled Penstemon

AMERICAN BROOKLIME; VERONICA

Veronica americana
Figwort Family (Scrophulariaceae)

Description: Sprawling, wavy-haired perennial, up to 10" long. The leaves are lanceolate, opposite, and 1–2" long. The inflorescence is a raceme of 4-lobed, saucer-shaped blue flowers. The flower is ½" wide and has an upper lobe that is wider than the other 3. The 2 stamens are exserted and the stigma is headlike.

May–August

Habitat/Range: Wetlands in mixed coniferous forest and subalpine forest.

Comments: The genus name possibly honors Saint Veronica, who swabbed Jesus' face with a cloth on his way to the crucifixion. The flower is thought to resemble the imprint of Christ's face on this cloth. The leaves and stems are edible and can be eaten raw.

American Brooklime; Veronica

Purple Nightshade

PURPLE NIGHTSHADE

Solanum xanti
Nightshade Family (Solanaceae)

Description: Hairy, often glandular perennial to subshrub up to 3' tall. The leaves are lanceolate to ovate and may have 1–2 lobes at the base. The inflorescence is an umbel-like cluster of saucer-shaped flowers, up to 1" wide. Each flower has 5 lobes with a tight cluster of bright yellow anthers in the center. The fruit is a smooth, green, poisonous berry.

May–September

Habitat/Range: Open areas in foothill woodland and mixed coniferous forest.

Comments: The genus name is Latin for "quieting," referring to the narcotic properties of some species. This plant is toxic. Members of this genus are pollinated when an insect, such as a bumblebee or hoverfly, uses its wings and thorax to set up a vibration in and around the anthers causing pollen to stream out, a process called "vibratory pollen collection."

KAREN WIESE

Western Dog Violet

WESTERN DOG VIOLET
Viola adunca
Violet Family (Violaceae)

Description: Perennial up to 8" tall. The leaves are round, 1 ½–2" long, and have wavy margins. The flowers are nodding, funnel shaped, and ½–¾" wide. Each blue-purple flower has 5 petals; 2 pointing upward, 2 hairy petals on the sides, and 1 petal on the bottom. The spurred bottom petal is larger than the others and has purple nectar guides that assist insects in locating nectar glands in the spur. The white hairs brush pollen off the insect directly onto the stigma, assisting pollination.

April–August

Habitat/Range: Wetlands in mixed coniferous forest and subalpine forest.

Comments: The genus name is the ancient Latin name for "violet," the color and the flower. The species name is Latin for "hooked," referring to the corolla. Some Native Americans, especially the Sierra Maidu, ate the stems and leaves as greens. They made a poultice from the leaves to relieve chest pains. The women chewed the roots to lessen pain during labor. Bumblebees and moths are the primary pollinators. The larvae of the great spangled fritillary (*Speyeria cybele*), the hydaspe fritillary (*S. hydaspe*), and the Pacific fritillary (*Boloria epithore*) butterflies feed on the leaves of violets.

Great Basin Violet

RICHARD HANES

GREAT BASIN VIOLET
Viola beckwithii
Violet Family (Violaceae)

Description: Perennial, 2–10" tall. The leaves are triangular, 2" long, and dissected into linear segments; the leaf stalk is 3" long and originates at the base of the plant. The nodding, funnel-shaped, 5-petaled flowers are ¾" long including the spur. The 2 upper petals are dark purple, and the lower 3 are fused into a spur and are lavender with a yellow inner area and purple nectar guides. The nectar guides attract pollinating insects to the nectar glands in the spur. The two lateral petals have yellow hairs that brush pollen off the insect pollinators directly onto the stigma.

March–August

Habitat/Range: Rocky, especially gravelly places in mixed coniferous forest, pinyon-juniper woodland, and sagebrush scrub, mostly on the east side of the Sierra Nevada.

Comments: In addition to bearing flowers that are bee and moth pollinated, violet plants also produce budlike, cleistogamous flowers, which are self-pollinating. These flowers ensure that seeds will be produced if pollinators are not present.

PINK FLOWERS

STEVE MATSON

This section includes flowers ranging from pale pink to deep magenta. Many species with pink flowers also have white flower variations. You may need to check the blue and purple, red, or white sections of this book if the flower you are searching for is not found here.

KAREN WIESE

Bitter Dogbane

BITTER DOGBANE
Apocynum androsaemifolium
Dogbane Family (Apocynaceae)

Description: Short, often spreading perennial 1' long, with milky sap. The leaves are opposite, drooping, ovate, with entire margins, and dark green above and pale below. The fragrant, bell-shaped corolla is ¼" long. The 2 tubular, ascending fruits have soft, tufted seeds inside that catch wind currents that disperse the seeds.

June–August

Habitat/Range: Open areas and rocky places in mixed coniferous forest.

Comments: The genus name is Greek for "away from dog," referring to its ancient use as a dog poison. The plant is also poisonous to humans and livestock. Some Native Americans used the stems as a source of fiber for rope.

SHOWY MILKWEED
Asclepias speciosa
Milkweed Family (Asclepiadaceae)

Description: Tall, hairy perennial with milky sap, up to 4' tall with opposite, clasping, elliptic to ovate leaves, 6" long. The inflorescence is an umbel of many unusual flowers. The 5 sepals are reflexed, and the 5 petals are lanceolate and spreading, exposing a crown of 5 concave hoods. The long fruit encloses many tiny, tufted seeds.

May–July

Habitat/Range: Open or shaded places in many habitats.

Comments: The genus name honors the ancient Greek physician and god of medicine, Asklepias. The species name is Latin for "showy," referring to the large, beautiful inflorescence. The stems of this plant yield a fiber that some Native Americans used for rope, nets, and basketry. Native Americans and settlers used the sap as an ingredient in a salve for warts, sores, and ringworm.

KAREN WIESE

Showy Milkweed

LYALL'S ROCK CRESS
Arabis lyallii
Mustard Family (Brassicaceae)

Description: Perennial up to 6" tall. The leaves are oblanceolate and up to 2" long. The flowers are only ⅜" long with 4 spoon-shaped petals. The fruits are 1–2 ¾" long.

July–August

Habitat/Range: Rocky places in subalpine forest and the alpine zone.

Comments: The genus name is Latin for "of Arabia"; this might refer the ability of plants in this genus to grow in rocky or sandy soils.

KAREN WIESE

Lyall's Rock Cress

KAREN WIESE

Beavertail Cactus

BEAVERTAIL CACTUS
Opuntia basilaris
Cactus Family (Cactaceae)

Description: Fleshy, perennial shrub covered with spines, ascending to erect, up to 16". The segments are flat, often with a white waxy or purplish cast. The flowers have many perianth parts with deep magenta-red filaments and a white stigma.

March–July

Habitat/Range: Open, dry areas in pinyon-juniper woodland in the southern Sierra Nevada.

Comments: The entire plant was used for food by Native Americans throughout the West. The segments were roasted to remove the spines, then sliced and eaten. The inside of the fruit can be scooped out and eaten or made into syrup or jam, though legislation now prevents collecting of any plant material without written permission from the landowner. The fruit, seeds, and stems are an important food source for wildlife.

KAREN CALLAHAN

Twin Flower

TWIN FLOWER
Linnaea borealis var. *longiflora*
Honeysuckle Family (Caprifoliaceae)

Description: Finely hairy perennial that trails up to 8". The margins of the ovate leaves are serrate midway to the tip. The inflorescence consists of 2 funnel-shaped flowers, each at the end of an erect 2" flower stem. The nodding corolla, ½" long, has 5 lobes.

June–August

Habitat/Range: Shaded areas in mixed coniferous forest.

Comments: The genus name honors the Swedish "Father of Botany," Carolus Linnaeus (1707–1778), founder of the binomial system of plant classification. The species name is Latin for "northern," referring to its circumboreal distribution.

WHITELEAF MANZANITA
Arctostaphylos viscida
Heath Family (Ericaceae)

Description: Shrub up to 16' tall. The many branches are deep maroon red. The ovate to round leaves are dull green and up to 1 ½" wide. The inflorescence is a cluster of many small, ⅜" long, urn-shaped, nodding flowers. The brown fruits look like tiny apples, hence the name *manzanita*, "little apples" in Spanish.

February–April

Habitat/Range: Open areas in foothill woodland and mixed coniferous forest.

Comments: The berrylike fruits are a valuable food source for wildlife; because bears like to eat them so much, the genus name is Greek for "bear berries." Some Native Americans ate the fresh berries raw and dried, and they used the pulp to make a cider. A skin tonic was made from the leaves to relieve the dermatitis associated with poison oak. The flowers are edible.

KAREN CALLAHAN

Whiteleaf Manzanita

BOG LAUREL
Kalmia polifolia ssp. *microphylla*
Heath Family (Ericaceae)

Description: Evergreen shrub 4–8" tall. The
¼–2" oblong leaves are opposite each other on
the stem. The saucer-shaped flowers are ¾"
across and have 5 petals fused at the base.

June–August

Habitat/Range: Rocky places and wetlands
in subalpine forest and the alpine zone.

Comments: The genus name honors Swedish botanist Peter Kalm (1716–1779), who was
a student of Linnaeus and traveled in eastern
North America. The subspecies name is Latin
for "small-leaved." The plant has 10 stamens
that, when triggered by an insect landing on
the flower, spring out of pockets in the petals
and discharge pollen. This plant is poisonous
to livestock.

Bog Laurel

Mountain Heather

MOUNTAIN HEATHER
Phyllodoce breweri
Heath Family (Ericaceae)

Description: Low-growing, multistemmed
evergreen shrub, up to 1' tall. The leaves are
linear and dense along the stem. The 5-pet-
aled, bell-shaped flowers are ½" across with
10 exserted stamens.

June–August

Habitat/Range: Wetlands and rocky places in
subalpine forest and the alpine zone.

Comments: The genus name honors the Greek
sea nymph mentioned by the Roman writer
Virgil and applies in a fanciful way to the flowers. The species name honors William H.
Brewer, the first person to botanize extensively
in the Sierra Nevada in the 1860s and collect
this plant in Yosemite in 1863. Brewer was
California's first state botanist and worked with
the California State Geological Survey.

Bog Wintergreen

BOG WINTERGREEN
Pyrola asarifolia
Heath Family (Ericaceae)

Description: Evergreen perennial up to 2' tall. The leaves are glossy, ovate to round, and basal. The flowers are nodding, borne on a leafless stalk, and have 5 petals and a downwardly curved, exserted style.

July–September

Habitat/Range: Dry areas to wetlands, especially moist stream banks, in mixed coniferous forest and subalpine forest.

Comments: Some Native Americans used this plant in various preparations to control swelling, particularly for insect bites and after childbirth. Another common name for this plant is shinleaf, referring to its use for inflammations.

HARLEQUIN LUPINE
Lupinus stiversii
Pea Family (Fabaceae)

Description: Annual up to 18" tall. The leaves are palmately compound with 6–8 leaflets, each up to 2" long. The inflorescence is a cluster of pea-family flowers, ¾" long. The banner is yellow, the wings are pink, and the keel is white. The fruit is brown, hairy, ¾" long, and filled with seeds.

April–July

Habitat/Range: Open areas in foothill woodland and mixed coniferous forest.

Comments: The common name, *harlequin*, means brightly colored. The species name honors Dr. Charles Austin Stivers of San Francisco, who in 1862 collected the plants near Yosemite National Park.

Harlequin Lupine

EDWARD RINGROSE

Whitney's Locoweed

WHITNEY'S LOCOWEED
Astragalus whitneyi
Pea Family (Fabaceae)

Description: Spreading or erect perennial, up to 16" tall. The leaves are compound and 4" long with 5–21 oblong leaflets. The inflorescence has 3–16 flowers, each a characteristic pea-family flower with a banner, ¾" tall, and a keel, ½" long. The flowers can be white, pink, or purple. The fruit looks like a papery bladder, 1 ½" long with red stripes.

May–September

Habitat/Range: Open areas and rocky places in subalpine forest, sagebrush scrub, pinyon-juniper woodland, and the alpine zone.

Comments: The genus name is Greek for "anklebone" or "dice." "Dice" may be more applicable, taking into account the rattling of the seeds in the pod. *Loco* means "crazy" in Spanish; this plant's alkaloid locoine damages the optic nerve of grazing animals, causing a disorientation in which the animals act "loco." The species name honors Josiah Dwight Whitney, who was the state geologist of California from 1860 to 1876 and made the first geologic study of Yosemite Valley. The larvae of the Melissa blue butterfly (*Lycaeides melissa*) feed on this plant.

Western Redbud

WESTERN REDBUD
Cercis occidentalis
Pea Family (Fabaceae)

Description: Tree, growing to 23' tall. The deciduous leaves are heart shaped, less than 4" long. The inflorescence is a cluster of pea-family flowers with keel petals ½" long. The oblong fruit is 3" long, red, and persistent.

February–April

Habitat/Range: Open areas in foothill woodland and mixed coniferous forest.

Comments: Some Native Americans used the bark to yield both red and tawny-colored basket weaving materials. The outer bark of the young shoots yielded a dark colored weaving material that was highly prized and traded. Some Native Americans made an astringent from the bark for a remedy for diarrhea and dysentery.

CALIFORNIA GERANIUM
Geranium californicum
Geranium Family (Geraniaceae)

Description: Erect, soft-hairy perennial, up to 2' tall, with white to yellow gland-tipped hairs along the stem. The leaves are round in outline, 2–12" long, and divided into 4–6 wedge-shaped segments. The upper ends of the segments are lobed. The 5-petaled, saucer-shaped flowers are 1" wide, with lavender to purple stripes. The fruit forms a narrow, pointed beak.

June–July

Habitat/Range: Wetlands in mixed coniferous forest and subalpine forest.

Comments: The genus name is Greek for "crane," referring to the fruit, which resembles a crane's bill. The "bill" is composed of 5 dried styles, each connected to a seed at the base. As the fruit dries, these sections twist and forcibly eject the seed. When the seed lands on the ground, the twisted column gets lodged in cracks in the ground, aiding in germination.

California Geranium

Nettleleaf Horsemint

NETTLELEAF HORSEMINT
Agastache urticifolia
Mint Family (Lamiaceae)

Description: Tall, aromatic perennial, 3–6' tall with a square stem. The leaves are opposite, triangular, and up to 3" long, with serrate margins. The inflorescence is a spike of many tubular flowers, each surrounded by a 5-lobed calyx that turns pink. Each flower is ½" long and has 2 lips. The upper lip is 2-lobed and the lower lip is longer, broader, and 3-lobed. There are 4 stamens with purple anthers that extend beyond the corolla.

June–August

Habitat/Range: Open areas in mixed coniferous forest, especially on meadow edges.

Comments: The genus name is Greek for "many spikes," referring to the spikelike inflorescence. The species name means "nettlelike leaf." Some Native Americans and herbalists have used the leaves to make a tea to induce sweating and expel gas.

TONY LOFTIN

Sierra Onion

SIERRA ONION
Allium campanulatum
Lily Family (Liliaceae)

Description: Perennial plant from a bulb, up to 1' tall. The 2–3 linear leaves are flat and thin, from the base of the plant. The inflorescence is an umbel of 10–50 flowers on a leafless stalk. Each flower has 3 petal-like sepals, 3 petals, and is ⅜" long. The perianth parts are lanceolate with a dark crescent at the base and can be pink or purple.

May–July

Habitat/Range: Open and sometimes semishaded dry areas in foothill woodland, mixed coniferous forest, and subalpine forest.

Comments: The genus name is Latin for "garlic." Some Native Americans ate the leaves and bulbs of this genus.

SWAMP ONION
Allium validum
Lily Family (Liliaceae)

Description: Perennial from a bulb, 1–3' tall. The 3–6 linear leaves are almost as tall as the flower stem. The inflorescence is an umbel of 15–40 flowers on a tall, leafless flower stalk. Each flower has 3 petal-like sepals and 3 petals. The perianth parts are lanceolate and ⅜" long. The stamens are exserted from the flower.

July–September

Habitat/Range: Wetlands in mixed coniferous forest, subalpine forest, and the alpine zone.

Comments: The species name is Latin for "strong," referring to the onionlike odor. The name "Onion Valley" has been used throughout the Sierra Nevada for meadows where early settlers found edible swamp onions.

KAREN WIESE

Swamp Onion

Red Sierra Onion

KAREN WIESE

RED SIERRA ONION
Allium obtusum
Lily Family (Liliaceae)

Description: Perennial from a bulb, up to 6" tall. The 1–2 linear leaves are flat and basal. The inflorescence is an umbel of 6–60 flowers that appear to sit on the ground, but are on a flower stalk that is ½" tall. Each flower is ⅜" long with 3 petal-like sepals and 3 petals. The perianth parts are lanceolate with purple midveins. The flower can be greenish white.

May–July

Habitat/Range: Open areas, especially in sandy soils, in foothill woodland, mixed coniferous forest, subalpine forest, and the alpine zone, especially in alpine fellfields.

Comments: The genus name is Latin for "garlic." Some Native Americans ate the leaves and bulbs of this genus.

RICHARD HANES

Butterfly Mariposa Lily; Square Mariposa Tulip

BUTTERFLY MARIPOSA LILY; SQUARE MARIPOSA TULIP
Calochortus venustus
Lily Family (Liliaceae)

Description: Perennial rising 2' from a bulb. The leaves, which wither away, are basal and 8" long. The inflorescence is a solitary flower or a cluster of 2–6 bell-shaped flowers. Each flower has 3 sepals and 3 petals. The petals can also be white, yellow, purple, or dark red. The erect, linear fruit is 3" long.

May–July

Habitat/Range: Open, sandy areas in foothill woodland and mixed coniferous forest.

Comments: The genus name is Greek for "beautiful grass," referring to this showy plant. The species name is Latin for "handsome" or "charming," referring to the flower. The Spanish named this plant *mariposa,* or "butterfly," referring to the colorful petals.

GREENHORN FRITILLARY
Fritillaria brandegei
Lily Family (Liliaceae)

Description: Perennial rising 3' from a bulb. The leaves are lanceolate, in 1–2 whorls of 4–8 below and alternate above. The nodding, bell-shaped flowers up to 1 ½" wide and have 3 petal-like sepals and 3 petals, which are lanceolate and pink to purple.

April–June

Habitat/Range: Open areas in granitic soils in mixed coniferous forest in the southern Sierra Nevada, especially the Greenhorn Mountains.

Comments: The genus name is Latin for "dice box," referring to the shape of the fruit. The species name honors early California botanists Townshend and Katherine Brandegee, who collected plants throughout California, Baja California, and western Nevada. This plant is rare.

NOEL LADUE

Greenhorn Fritillary

WHITE-VEINED MALLOW
Sidalcea glaucescens
Mallow Family (Malvaceae)

Description: Slender, whitish-waxy perennial up to 2' tall. The leaves are deeply lobed into 5–7 divisions. The inflorescence is an open raceme, with flowers along one side of the top of the plant. The flowers are ⅜–⅝" wide and saucer shaped, with 5 petals and with many stamens fused at the base. The fruit has 5–10 wedge-shaped segments arranged like the spokes of a wheel.

May–July

Habitat/Range: Open areas in foothill woodland and mixed coniferous forest.

Comments: The genus name is a combination of two Latin words for "mallow," sida and alcea. The early settlers applied them as a poultice to ease the pain of insect stings and to draw out thorns and splinters.

White-Veined Mallow

Bog Mallow

BOG MALLOW
Sidalcea oregana
Mallow Family (Malvaceae)

Description: Perennial up to 3' tall. The leaves are mostly basal, round in outline, with scalloped edges. The inflorescence is a spike of open, funnel-shaped flowers, up to 1" wide. Each flower has 5 petals, often notched at the outer edge.

June–August

Habitat/Range: Wetlands in mixed coniferous forest, subalpine forest, pinyon-juniper woodland, and sagebrush scrub.

Comments: At one time, the thick sap of a species that grows in the eastern United States was mixed with sugar and used in making marshmallows.

KAREN CALLAHAN

Rhomboid-Leaf Clarkia;Tongue Clarkia

RHOMBOID-LEAF CLARKIA; TONGUE CLARKIA
Clarkia rhomboidea
Evening-Primrose Family (Onagraceae)

Description: Annual up to 3' tall. The leaves are lanceolate, ½–1 ½" long, and opposite. The flower buds are nodding. The flowers are ¾" wide, saucer shaped, with 4 petals. The petals are shaped like a rhomboid or diamond. The sepals are reflexed. The stigma is 4-lobed. The flowers close at night and open the next day; each blossom lasts several days.

May–July

Habitat/Range: Open areas in foothill woodland and mixed coniferous forest.

Comments: The genus name honors Captain William Clark (1770–1838) of the 1804–1806 Lewis and Clark Expedition. The seeds of *Clarkia* species were among the most highly prized foods of some Native Americans in the Sierra Nevada, especially the Miwok tribes. When ripe, the tops of the plants were tied in bundles and dried on rocks. After they had dried, the plants were unbundled and the seeds were dislodged by beating with a stick. The seeds were parched and ground into meal that was eaten dry or with acorn meal.

DANN MCCRIGHT

Elegant Clarkia

ELEGANT CLARKIA
Clarkia unguiculata
Evening-Primrose Family (Onagraceae)

Description: Annual plant with a white waxy coating up to 3' tall. The leaves are lanceolate and up to 2" long. The flower buds are nodding. The flower is saucer shaped, up to 1" long, with 4 triangular petals that each have a narrow base, which is called a "claw." The flower can be pink, lavender, salmon, or dark red-violet. The stigma is 4-lobed and extends beyond the anthers. The outer 4 of the 8 anthers are red.

May–June

Habitat/Range: Shaded areas in foothill woodland and mixed coniferous forest.

Comments: The species name means "clawed," referring to the narrow stalk at the base of the petals.

KAREN CALLAHAN

Fireweed

FIREWEED
Epilobium angustifolium ssp. *circumvagum*
Evening-Primrose Family (Onagraceae)

Description: Perennial, 2–6' tall. The leaves are alternate, lanceolate, and 3–8" long. The flower buds are nodding. The inflorescence is a long raceme of many flowers. Each flower is 1" wide, with 4 obovate petals that alternate with green triangular sepals. The flowers open up from the bottom of the raceme to the top. The stigma becomes 4-parted when receptive to pollination. The fruit is 1 ½–4" long and splits into four parts, releasing tiny tufted seeds when mature.

July–September

Habitat/Range: Open areas in foothill woodland, mixed coniferous forest, subalpine forest, and the alpine zone.

Comments: The genus name is Greek for "upon a pod," referring to the position of the flower on a seedpod. Botanists call this arrangement an "inferior ovary," meaning that the ovary is below the corolla. The common name refers to both the flaming color of flower and foliage as it ages, and the fact that the plant is one of the first to become established after a disturbance such as fire. The seeds, which have fuzzy tufts, are easily dispersed by wind. Some Native Americans ate the young leaves as greens as an early spring source of vitamin C; they also ate the peeled stems.

ROCK FRINGE
Epilobium obcordatum
Evening-Primrose Family (Onagraceae)

Description: Cushionlike perennial up to 6" long. The leaves are elliptic to round, ¾" long, and crowded and opposite on the stem. The inflorescence has 1 to several flowers, 1" wide and large in relation to the plant, with 4 lobed petals. The velvety, dark pink stigma extends beyond the corolla and is 4-lobed when receptive to pollen.

July–September

Habitat/Range: Rocky places in subalpine forest and the alpine zone.

Comments: The species name is Latin for "heart-shaped," referring to the petals. As the common name implies, rock fringe grows huddled in rock crevices.

Rock Fringe

Striped Coralroot

STRIPED CORALROOT
Corallorhiza striata
Orchid Family (Orchidaceae)

Description: Perennial with a red-brown to purple stem, 6–20" tall. The inflorescence is a raceme of up to 45 striped flowers along a leafless stem. The flowers are up to 1" wide and ½" long. The 3 sepals are yellow-pink to pale brown, with red stripes. The lateral petals are sepal-like, and the center petal is elliptic and white with purple stripes. This flower can appear dull yellow.

May–July

Habitat/Range: Open areas in decomposing leaf litter in mixed coniferous forest and subalpine forest, especially red fir forests.

Comments: The genus name is Greek for "coral root"; the root of this plant looks like a multibranched sea coral. The species name is Latin for "striped," referring to the striped flower. Striped coralroot is the first wild orchid to bloom in the Sierra.

KAREN CALLAHAN

Stream Orchid

STREAM ORCHID
Epipactis gigantea
Orchid Family (Orchidaceae)

Description: Perennial, 1–2' tall. The leaves are lanceolate to widely elliptic, occur along the stem, and are smaller toward the top of the plant. The inflorescence can have 12–18 flowers on one flower stalk, usually facing the same direction. The flowers are up to 1 ¾" wide. The 3 sepals are green with purple veins. The 2 lateral petals are pink to red-purple. The center petal forms a lip that is lobed and concave, green to yellow, and veined red-purple. The flower has many color variations.

May–August

Habitat/Range: Wetlands, especially moist stream banks, in foothill woodland, mixed coniferous forest, subalpine forest, pinyon-juniper woodland, and sagebrush scrub.

Comments: The species name is Latin for "gigantic," referring to the flower size. The flowers have a sweet aroma, which attracts flies in the Syrphidae family. The aroma of this plant mimics that of honeydew, the sugary secretion given off by aphids. Syrphid flies normally lay their eggs amidst aphids, which become food for their larvae. In this case, however, the fly is fooled into laying its eggs inside the flower; as it does so, it picks up pollen, which it then deposits on the next flower.

BLEEDING HEART
Dicentra formosa
Poppy Family (Papaveraceae)

Description: Perennial, 8–18" tall. The finely dissected leaves are 8–20" long and occur at the base of the plant. The inflorescence has 4 or more flowers per plant in a nodding cluster. Each nodding flower has 4 petals fused in the shape of a heart.

March–July

Habitat/Range: Shaded places in foothill woodland and mixed coniferous forest.

Comments: The genus name is Greek for "two-spurred," referring to the flower. The species name is Latin for "beautiful." The larvae of the Clodius Parnassian butterfly (*Parnassius clodius*) feed on this plant. This host plant contains poisonous alkaloids that make this butterfly bitter and poisonous to predators such as birds.

Bleeding Heart

Steer's Head

STEER'S HEAD
Dicentra uniflora
Poppy Family (Papaveraceae)

Description: Perennial, 1–3" tall, that blooms immediately after snowmelt. The 1–3 leaves are finely dissected, 2" long. Each plant has 1 nodding flower with ½" petals. The outermost petals are recurved into the shape of the horns of a steer, and the other two petals are fused into the shape of a steer's head.

May–July

Habitat/Range: Open and rocky areas in mixed coniferous forest and subalpine forest.

Comments: The genus name is from the Greek for "two-spurred," referring to the flower. The species name means "one-flowered," referring to the plant's single flower.

Slender Gilia

SLENDER GILIA
Gilia leptalea
Phlox Family (Polemoniaceae)

Description: Slightly glandular annual, often branched, up to 1' tall, forming carpets of flowers. The leaves are linear and ½–2" long. The inflorescence is composed of loose, spreading, funnel-shaped flowers less than ½" wide, with a purple or yellow throat, a yellow corolla tube, and pink or purple outer lobes. The 3-parted stigma and the stamens are exserted from the corolla. The pollen of this plant is blue. This flower can also appear purple.

June–August

Habitat/Range: Open areas and rocky places in mixed coniferous forest and subalpine forest, often in meadows.

Comments: The genus name honors the Spanish botanist Felipe Gil (1756–1821). The species name is Latin for "slender," referring to the plant. This plant is also referred to as Bridges' gilia.

WHISKER-BRUSH
Linanthus ciliatus
Phlox Family (Polemoniaceae)

Description: Hairy annual, up to 1' tall, often forming colonies. The leaves are bristly, linear, ¾" long, and in whorls around the stem. The inflorescence is a spherical cluster of bristly bracts, ½" long, with trumpet-shaped flowers sticking out of the sphere. The 5-lobed corolla is ¼" wide with a yellow throat and a purple triangle at the base of each petal lobe.

May–July

Habitat/Range: Open and shaded areas in foothill woodland, mixed coniferous forest, and subalpine forest.

Comments: The genus name is Greek for "flax flower"; this plant's flower resembles that of a flax. The species name is Latin for "fringed," referring to the hairy leaf edges. Whisker-brush is named for the arrangement of the bracts and leaves, which resemble a shaving brush.

Whisker-Brush

SPREADING PHLOX
Phlox diffusa
Phlox Family (Polemoniaceae)

Description: Matted perennial with sprawling stems, 4–12" long. The leaves are linear and opposite, lacking sharp tips. The fragrant flowers are trumpet shaped, up to ½" wide, and occur in masses on each plant. The corolla can also be white, lavender, or blue.

June–August

Habitat/Range: Open areas and rocky places in mixed coniferous forest, subalpine forest, and the alpine zone.

Comments: The genus name is Greek for "a flame," referring to the brilliant flower colors of other species in this genus. The species name is Latin for "spreading," referring to the growth habit of this plant.

Spreading Phlox

Wright's Buckwheat

WRIGHT'S BUCKWHEAT
Eriogonum wrightii
Buckwheat Family (Polygonaceae)

Description: Matted, many branched subshrub, up to 1' tall. The linear to elliptic leaves occur clustered mostly low on the stem. The leaves are woolly beneath. The inflorescence is a cluster of small flowers on an often woolly flower stem. The 6 petal-like sepals can be pink or white.

July–October

Habitat/Range: Rocky places in mixed coniferous forest, subalpine forest, and pinyon-juniper woodland.

Comments: The genus name is Greek for "wool knee," referring to the hairy nodes of many species.

KAREN WIESE

Pussypaws

PUSSYPAWS
Calyptridium umbellatum
Purslane Family (Portulacaceae)

Description: Erect to sprawling perennial up to 2' tall, often only 10". The oblanceolate leaves, 1–3" long, are in basal rosettes. There are 2–10 flower stems, 1–8" long, that radiate from the base of the plant. At the end of each flower stem is the inflorescence, a spherical cluster of flowers, up to 2" wide. The tiny, 4-petaled flowers can be pink or white, but it is the 2 broad sepals and the papery bracts, ¼" long, that make the flower heads colorful.

May–August

Habitat/Range: Open areas, especially sandy and rocky soils, in mixed coniferous forest, subalpine forest, and the alpine zone.

Comments: The genus name is Greek for "cap" or "veil," referring to the way the petals close over the seed capsule with age. The species name refers to the umbrella-like flower stem. "Pussypaws" comes from the soft feel and pawlike shape of the inflorescence. The stems of this plant thermoregulate, which means they respond to temperature. When it is cool, in the evening and morning, the stems lay flat on the ground, protected from chilling winds. As the day warms, the flower stems rise, absorbing the midday warmth, but moving away from the scorching soil. The tiny black seeds are an important source of food for rodents.

WIN & BOB EHRHART

Lewisia; Bitterroot

LEWISIA; BITTERROOT
Lewisia rediviva
Purslane Family (Portulacaceae)

Description: Fleshy perennial up to 2" tall, with many linear leaves in a basal rosette. The inflorescence is a solitary flower, 1 ½" wide, on a 1–2" flower stalk. There may be 1 to many flowers, each with 6–8 sepals that look like petals plus 10–19 petals. The flowers may be pink, white, rose, or purple.

March–June

Habitat/Range: Rocky places in foothill woodland, mixed coniferous forest, pinyon-juniper woodland, and sagebrush shrub.

Comments: The genus name honors Meriwether Lewis (1774–1809), explorer and leader of the 1804–1806 Lewis and Clark Expedition. The species name is Latin for "restored, brought to life," referring to the dried specimens that were grown by Bernard McMahon, a nurseryman from Philadelphia, from a root removed from a dried herbarium specimen collected during the Lewis and Clark Expedition of 1804–1806. The common name refers to the bitter covering on the roots. Some Native Americans ate the roots after soaking and cooking them by boiling, roasting, or steaming in a fire pit. The bitter outer rind was removed and the roots were eaten cooked, or dried and ground into meal.

Alpine Shooting Star

ALPINE SHOOTING STAR
Dodecatheon alpinum
Primrose Family (Primulaceae)

Description: Perennial up to 1' tall. The leaves are linear to oblanceolate, basal, 1–8" long, and narrowed gradually to the base. The inflorescence is an umbel of 1–10 flowers on a stalk. The nodding flowers have 4 petals that are reflexed, exposing pointed black stamens. The petals are ⅜–1" long and can be magenta or lavender. The bases of the petals are maroon, with a yellow band above. The stigma tip extends beyond the stamens. After pollination, the nodding flowers become erect. The petals fall off and the once-hidden sepals fold up to protect the seed capsule.

July–August

Habitat/Range: Wetlands in mixed coniferous forest, subalpine forest, and the alpine zone.

Comments: The genus name is Greek for "twelve gods," referring to the flowers, which sometimes appear in clusters of twelve. The Roman naturalist Pliny (A.D. 23–79) bestowed this name because he thought the flowers represented the twelve Olympian gods.

CAROL GRENIER

Sierra Primrose

SIERRA PRIMROSE
Primula suffrutescens
Primrose Family (Primulaceae)

Description: Sprawling, perennial subshrub up to 5" tall. The spoon-shaped, evergreen leaves, 3–5" long, have serrate leaf margins and occur mostly as a basal rosette. The inflorescence is an umbel of 5-petaled, trumpet-shaped flowers, ½–¾" wide. The corolla is magenta with a yellow throat.

July–August

Habitat/Range: Rocky places in subalpine forest and the alpine zone.

Comments: The genus name is Latin for "very first," referring to the early bloom of this flower. The species name is Latin for "somewhat shrubby," referring to the woody base. This plant was first collected in Yosemite in 1872 by the American botanist Asa Gray (1810–1888). His guides were the naturalist John Muir (1835–1914) and mountaineer Galen Clark.

KAREN CALLAHAN

Starflower

STARFLOWER
Trientalis latifolia
Primrose Family (Primulaceae)

Description: Delicate perennial up to 1' tall. The leaves are ovate, 1–3 ½" long, and whorled at the top of the plant, just below the flower. The 5–7 petaled, star-shaped flower, ⅜–½" wide, is centered above the leaves. The flower can also be white.

April–July

Habitat/Range: Shaded places in mixed coniferous forest, frequently in redwood forests.

Comments: The genus name is Latin for "one-third of a foot," referring to the height of the plant. The species name is Latin for "broad-leaved."

OLD MAN'S WHISKERS; DOWNY AVENS
Geum triflorum
Rose Family (Rosaceae)

Description: Perennial, 8–20" tall. The leaves are pinnate, lobed, and 2–8" long. The inflorescence has 1–3 nodding flowers, ½" long and bell shaped, which can be white or pink. After fertilization, the petals and sepals fall away, and each seed head becomes erect and has many feathery reddish styles, up to 1 ½" long, that are attached to seeds.

June–August

Habitat/Range: Open areas, especially meadow edges, in mixed coniferous forest, sub-alpine forest, and sagebrush scrub.

Comments: The genus name is the Latin name for this plant. The species name is Latin for "three-flowered," referring to the three flowers in the inflorescence. "Old man's whiskers" comes from the whiskerlike cluster of styles.

LAURIE FRIEDMAN

Old Man's Whiskers; Downy Avens

INTERIOR ROSE
Rosa woodsii var. *ultramontana*
Rose Family (Rosaceae)

Description: Prickly, thicket-forming shrub, 3–9' tall. The leaves are compound, with 5–7 elliptic, serrate leaflets. The inflorescence has 1–5, 5-petaled flowers, 1–2" wide and very fragrant with numerous pistils and stamens. The fruit, a rose hip, grows to ½" wide and has many seeds inside.

June–August

Habitat/Range: Wetlands in mixed coniferous forest, particularly on the east side of the Sierra Nevada.

Comments: The genus name is the ancient Latin name for "rose," the word our English term is derived from as well. Some Native Americans gathered the rose hips, which are high in vitamin C, in the fall and ate them raw or made a tea out of them.

Interior Rose

KAREN WIESE

MOUNTAIN SPIRAEA
Spiraea densiflora
Rose Family (Rosaceae)

Description: Deciduous shrub up to 3' tall. The leaves are elliptic, up to 3" long, and serrate. The inflorescence is a wide, flat-topped cluster of many small flowers. The many stamens extend beyond the petals, giving the flower head a soft, fluffy appearance.

July–August

Habitat/Range: Rocky, especially moist places in mixed coniferous forest and subalpine forest.

Comments: The genus name is from the Greek word for a "band" or "wreath," referring to a plant in this genus that was used in garlands. The species name is Latin for "dense-flowered."

KAREN WIESE

Mountain Spiraea

Pink Heuchera; Alumroot

KAREN WIESE

PINK HEUCHERA; ALUMROOT
Heuchera rubescens
Saxifrage Family (Saxifragaceae)

Description: Perennial up to 20" tall. The leaves are basal and occur at the end of a leaf stem. The outline of the leaf is circular, up to 2 ½" wide, with 5–9 deep lobes. The flowers are glandular and occur in an open raceme; each flower is ⅓" long and bell shaped, with 5 narrow petals that can be pink or white. The 5 stamens and 2 styles are exserted from the flower.

May–July

Habitat/Range: Shaded areas and rocky places in mixed coniferous forest, subalpine forest, pinyon-juniper woodland, and the alpine zone.

Comments: The genus name honors the German professor of medicine Johann H. von Heucher (1677–1747).

LEMMON'S PAINTBRUSH
Castilleja lemmonii
Figwort Family (Scrophulariaceae)

Description: Hairy, glandular perennial, 4–8" tall. The leaves are linear to lanceolate and ¾–1 ½" long. The inflorescence is a spike, 1–5" long, with magenta bracts and calyx parts. The 2-lipped tubular flower is ¾" long and yellow.

July–August

Habitat/Range: Wetlands, especially moist meadows, in subalpine forest and the alpine zone.

Comments: The species name honors John G. Lemmon (1832–1908), who, with his wife, Sara Plummer Lemmon, collected plants throughout the western United States.

KAREN WIESE

Lemmon's Paintbrush

LEWIS'S MONKEYFLOWER
Mimulus lewisii
Figwort Family (Scrophulariaceae)

Description: Glandular, hairy perennial, 1–3′ tall. The leaves are opposite, oblong, ¾–3″ long, and often clasp the stem. The flowers occur in pairs in the axils of the upper leaves. The 5-lobed, 2-lipped, trumpet-shaped flowers are 1–2″ long, with the upper lip curved upward and the lower lip reflexed. The throat floor of the corolla has yellow ridges with white hairs. The yellow color attracts pollinators and acts as a nectar guide. The hairs aid in brushing pollen off of pollinators.

June–September

Habitat/Range: Wetlands, especially stream banks and seeps, in mixed coniferous forest.

Comments: The species name honors Meriwether Lewis (1774–1809), explorer and leader of the 1804–1806 Lewis and Clark Expedition.

Lewis's Monkeyflower

LAYNE'S MONKEYFLOWER
Mimulus layneae
Figwort Family (Scrophulariaceae)

Description: Hairy annual, 1–11″ tall. The leaves are opposite, elliptic, and up to 1 ½″ long. The flowers occur in pairs in the axils of the upper leaves. The 5-lobed, 2-lipped, trumpet-shaped flowers are ½–¾″ long. The upper lip is reflexed.

May–August

Habitat/Range: Open areas in mixed coniferous forest.

Layne's Monkeyflower

Copeland's Owl's-Clover

LAURIE FRIEDMAN

COPELAND'S OWL'S-CLOVER
Orthocarpus cuspidatus ssp. *cryptanthus*
Figwort Family (Scrophulariaceae)

Description: Hairy annual, 4–16" tall. The leaves are alternate, lanceolate, and up to 2" long. The inflorescence is a 1–4" spike of dense, ovate, petal-like bracts. The tips of the bracts are pink. Hidden among the bracts are tubular, hairy flowers, ½–1" long. Each flower has a pink upper lip, which is beaklike and covers the anthers and style, and a white lower lip, with 3 small teeth.

June–August

Habitat/Range: Open areas in subalpine forest and sagebrush scrub.

Comments: The genus name is Greek for "straight fruit," referring to the linear fruit of some species. This plant is a partial parasite, obtaining some of its water and minerals by attaching its roots to the roots of other plants.

LITTLE ELEPHANT'S HEAD
Pedicularis attollens
Figwort Family (Scrophulariaceae)

Description: Perennial, partial root parasite, up to 2' tall. The deeply lobed, almost fern-like, leaves are linear in outline, basal, and sometimes reaching 8" long. The inflorescence is a spike of many densely clustered and hairy flowers. The flowers are ⅜" long, pink to purple, and shaped like the head of an elephant, with the 2 upper petals fused into a short "trunk" and the 3-lobed lower petals forming the "ears."

June–September

Habitat/Range: Wetlands in mixed coniferous forest, subalpine forest, and the alpine zone.

Comments: This plant is similar to elephant's head (*P. groenlandica*) except for the smaller leaves and flowers, the shorter trunk that curves down like a sickle, and the hairy flowers. The little elephant's head will also bloom later into the season.

Little Elephant's Head

DANN MCCRIGHT

Elephant's Head

ELEPHANT'S HEAD
Pedicularis groenlandica
Figwort Family (Scrophulariaceae)

Description: Perennial, partial root parasite, up to 30" tall. The deeply lobed, almost fern-like leaves are basal, sometimes reaching 10" long. The inflorescence is a spike of many densely clustered flowers. The flowers are ½" long, dark pink, and shaped like the head of an elephant, with the 2 upper petals fused into a long "trunk" and the 3-lobed lower petals forming the "ears."

June–August

Habitat/Range: Wetlands in mixed coniferous forest, subalpine forest, and the alpine zone.

Comments: The genus name is Latin for "louse," referring to the belief that livestock that ate this plant would get lice. Livestock that graze on these plants may become under-nourished and more susceptible to ectoparasites such as lice because the nutrient value in its forage is poor. The plant is a partial parasite, obtaining some of its water and minerals from a host plant. The species name is Latin for "of Greenland," referring to another geographic location where it is found. This plant is circumboreal—it is found throughout the world in northern latitudes. The flower is bee pollinated.

DANN MCCRIGHT

Mountain Pride Penstemon

MOUNTAIN PRIDE PENSTEMON
Penstemon newberryi
Figwort Family (Scrophulariaceae)

Description: Mat-forming subshrub 6–12" tall that forms brilliant displays along rocky crevices. The leaves are opposite, ovate, mostly basal, up to 1 ½" long, and finely serrate. The flowers occur in pairs in the axils of the upper leaves. Each 2-lipped, tubular flower is 1" long; the upper lip has 2 lobes, and the lower lip has 3 lobes. The throat floor of the corolla has yellow, hairy ridges that act as nectar guides for pollinators and pollen-collecting brushes for pollinators. The flower has 4 stamens and 1 pale yellow, hairy staminode ¾ the length of the stamens.

June–August

Habitat/Range: Rocky places in mixed coniferous forest and subalpine forest.

Comments: *Penstemon* is the largest genus of flowering plants endemic to North America. There are over 250 species in North America, with 50 in California. The species name honors John Strong Newberry (1822–1892), a botanist, geologist, and paleontologist who collected in California on the Williamson Railroad Survey.

Red and Orange Flowers

This section includes flowers ranging from pale orange to deep red and burgundy. Many species of flowers will turn orange, red, or burgundy as they age. If these flowers were once white or yellow when they were young, you may need to check those sections if the flower you are looking for is not here.

Anderson's Thistle

ANDERSON'S THISTLE
Cirsium andersonii
Aster Family (Asteraceae)

Description: Spiny perennial that grows 12–40" tall. The leaves have spiny-winged leaf stalks and are usually green above and gray-hairy on the underside. Each plant has 1 to several flower heads that are cylindrical to bell shaped and protected by spines. The corolla is 1–1 ¾" long.

June–October

Habitat/Range: Open or shaded places in mixed coniferous forest.

Comments: The genus name is an ancient Greek word for "swollen vein," referring to an extract that was made from thistles to treat swollen veins. Some Native Americans ate the roots, leaves, and stems raw or cooked.

CALIFORNIA INDIAN PINK
Silene californica
Pink Family (Caryophyllaceae)

Description: Prostrate perennial with several stems, 8–20" long. The leaves are ovate, 3" long, and occur along the stem. The trumpet-shaped flowers are 1–2" wide and have 5 petals that each have 4–6 lobes.

March–August

Habitat/Range: Shaded areas in foothill woodland and mixed coniferous forest.

Comments: The genus name is thought to be derived from the Greek myth of Silenus, the intoxicated foster-father of Bacchus (god of wine), who was covered with foam, much like the glandular secretions of many species of *Silene*, including this one.

California Indian Pink

LIVE-FOREVER
Dudleya cymosa
Stonecrop Family (Crassulaceae)

Description: Succulent perennial up to 18" tall, with a red flower stem. The leaves are oblanceolate, up to 7" long, and form a basal rosette up to 8" wide. The inflorescence is a cluster of 4–20 star-shaped, 5-petaled flowers ¼–½" long on a flower stalk that rises from the side of the basal rosette. The flowers can be red or yellow.

April–June

Habitat/Range: Rocky outcrops in foothill woodland and mixed coniferous forest.

Comments: The genus name honors W. R. Dudley (1849–1911), professor of botany at Stanford University, who studied the plants of the western United States. The leaves of members of the genus *Dudleya* were considered a delicacy by some Native Americans and were consumed raw.

LAURIE FRIEDMAN

Live-Forever

KAREN WIESE

Rosy Sedum

ROSY SEDUM
Sedum roseum ssp. *integrifolium*
Stonecrop Family (Crassulaceae)

Description: Fleshy perennial with several stems, up to 6" tall. The leaves are flat, obovate, ¼–1" long, and equally distributed along the stem. The inflorescence is 1" wide, a dense cluster of 7–50 small, star-shaped flowers. Each flower has 4 or 5 tiny petals. The anthers are light brown to red-purple.

June–August

Habitat/Range: Rocky places in mixed coniferous forest, subalpine forest, and the alpine zone.

Comments: The species name is Latin for "rose-colored," referring to the leaves. Some Native Americans gathered this plant in late fall and early spring and ate the cooked roots.

KAREN WIESE

Snow Plant

SNOW PLANT
Sarcodes sanguinea
Heath Family (Ericaceae)

Description: Fleshy perennial, 1' tall. The leaves are scalelike, lanceolate, and up to 3" long. There are up to 30 nodding, urn-shaped flowers on a 1–2" thick, stout stalk. Each flower is ¾" long with 5 fused petals.

May–July

Habitat/Range: Shaded areas in mixed coniferous forest and subalpine forest, especially red fir.

Comments: In spite of its common name, snow plant does not come up through snow. The genus name is Greek for "fleshlike," referring to the inflorescence. The species name is Latin for "blood-red," referring to the plant's overall color. This plant does not photosynthesize; instead, it derives its nutrients through a relationship with soil fungi. Some Native Americans dried and ground this plant into a powder to relieve toothaches and other mouth pains.

SCARLET FRITILLARY
Fritillaria recurva
Lily Family (Liliaceae)

Description: Perennial, 1–3' tall, from a bulb. The leaves are linear, 1–6" long, and in whorls of 2–5 leaves or alternate along the stem. The often nodding, bell-shaped flowers are ½–1 ½" long with 3 petal-like sepals and 3 petals. The flowers are scarlet, checkered with yellow on the inside and purple on the outside of the perianth parts. The tips of the perianth parts are recurved.

March–July

Habitat/Range: Shaded areas in foothill woodland and mixed coniferous forest.

Comments: The species name is Latin for "recurved," referring to the petal and sepal tips.

NOEL LADUE

Scarlet Fritillary

Leopard Lily; Panther Lily

LEOPARD LILY; PANTHER LILY

Lilium pardalinum
Lily Family (Liliaceae)

Description: Perennial rising up to 8' from a bulb, forming masses in moist places. The leaves are elliptic, arranged in whorls along the stem. As many as 35 nodding flowers bloom on each plant. Each trumpet-shaped flower has 3 petal-like sepals and 3 petals, 2–4" long, which are recurved and two-toned with yellow-orange at the base and red at the tips. Each perianth segment has maroon spots in the middle that attract pollinating insects.

May–July

Habitat/Range: Wetlands in mixed coniferous forest.

Comments: The genus name is the ancient Latin word for "lily," a term that probably came from the same ancient source as the Greek word for lily, *lirion*—Europeans have known this group of plants since antiquity. The species name is Latin for "leopard," referring to the spots on the perianth parts. Some Native Americans roasted the bulbs for food.

Alpine Lily

ALPINE LILY
Lilium parvum
Lily Family (Liliaceae)

Description: Perennial rising up to 6" from a bulb. The leaves are lanceolate, 1 ½–6" long, and occur along the stem or in whorls. As many as 41 ascending or occasionally nodding, trumpet-shaped flowers bloom on each plant. The flowers are 1–1 ½" long and have 3 petal-like sepals and 3 petals, which are all slightly recurved. Inside the flower are maroon spots that act as nectar guides for pollinating insects.

June–September

Habitat/Range: Wetlands, especially alder and willow thickets, in mixed coniferous forest and subalpine forest.

Comments: The genus name is the classical name for "lily." The species name is Latin for "small," referring to the flower.

SPOTTED CORALROOT
Corallorhiza maculata
Orchid Family (Orchidaceae)

Description: Perennial, 7–21" tall, with a red to yellow-brown stem. The inflorescence is a raceme of 20–30 flowers along the stem. The flowers are about ¾" wide and ⅜" long with 3 red sepals and 2 red lateral petals. The white center petal looks like a 3-lobed lip with red spots.

May–August

Habitat/Range: Open and shaded areas in decomposing leaf litter in mixed coniferous forest and subalpine forest.

Comments: The genus name is Greek for "coral root"; the root of this plant resembles a multibranched sea coral. The species name is Latin for "spotted," referring to the spotted center petal. This plant does not photosynthesize; it obtains nutrients through a relationship with soil fungi.

Spotted Coralroot

EDWARD RINGROSE

California Fuchsia

CALIFORNIA FUCHSIA
Epilobium canum
Evening-Primrose Family (Onagraceae)

Description: Dense, hairy perennial to sub-shrub, up to 3' long, often sprawling. The leaves are ½–2" long, gray-green, ovate, and opposite. The inflorescence is a cluster of 1–2" tubular flowers that have 4 petals with slightly notched tips. The 4-lobed stigma and the stamens extend beyond the corolla.

August–September

Habitat/Range: Open areas and rocky places in foothill woodland, mixed coniferous forest, and subalpine forest.

Comments: This is one of the latest wildflowers to bloom; therefore, it is a major nectar source for hummingbirds on their southward migration. Nectar glands, positioned at the base of the corolla, insure that each feeding hummingbird will brush up against the exserted stamens and deposit pollen on the stigma. Some Native Americans used the leaves to make a tea to relieve kidney and bladder ailments. This plant used to be called *Zauschneria californica.*

DANN MCCRIGHT

Wild Peony

WILD PEONY
Paeonia brownii
Peony Family (Paeoniaceae)

Description: Perennial 8–16" tall. The 5–8 leaves are blue-green, deeply dissected, and 1–2" long. Each plant has 1 to several nodding flowers, 1" wide, at the end of each stem. The corolla has 5 or 6 green sepals that are persistent and larger than the petals, which are leathery, rounded, and maroon with a yellow tinge. The plant has many stamens born on a fleshy disk; the stamens mature from the center outward. The 2–5 pistils each mature to a large fruit ¾–1 ½" long; each fruit holds a few seeds. The fruit may be the only part of the plant to see, because the flower blooms early.

April–June

Habitat/Range: Open areas in mixed coniferous forest and sagebrush scrub.

Comments: The genus honors Paeon, mythological physician to the gods in Homer's *Iliad* who used the plant to heal the wound that Hercules inflicted on Pluto. The Washoe and Paiute tribes made a tea from the roots to treat lung problems. The peony is bee pollinated, offering no nectar, but abundant pollen.

California Poppy

CALIFORNIA POPPY
Eschscholzia californica
Poppy Family (Papaveraceae)

Description: Annual and sometimes perennial, up to 2' tall, with an erect to sprawling growth form. The leaves are blue-green, finely dissected, and arranged alternately mostly at the base of the stem. The broad, funnel-shaped flowers are 2–3" across with 4 wedge-shaped petals. The flower has many stamens, which produce pollen that bees collect. The flowers fold up during the night and on cloudy days, protecting their pollen from harmful moisture and therefore allowing bees, which pollinate during the day, to gather more pollen. A flat receptacle disk remains when the petals fall off. Below this disk, the slender, conical fruits are 1 ½–3" long and filled with many tiny "poppy" seeds.

February–September

Habitat/Range: Open areas in foothill woodland and mixed coniferous forest.

Comments: This plant became California's state flower in 1903. The genus name honors the Russian surgeon and naturalist Johann Friedrich Gustav von Eschscholtz (1793–1831). Some Native Californians used the leaves and roots, which are mildly sedative and analgesic (pain killing), for toothaches, headaches, spastic colon, and gallbladder ailments. They also fried the flower petals in bear grease to make a hair oil and cooked the leaves for greens.

KAREN WIESE

Large-Flowered Collomia

LARGE-FLOWERED COLLOMIA
Collomia grandiflora
Phlox Family (Polemoniaceae)

Description: Hairy, glandular annual up to 3' tall. The leaves are alternate, lanceolate, and 1–2" long. The inflorescence is a 2" wide sphere of trumpet-shaped flowers, each ½–1" long. The pollen of this flower is blue.

April–July

Habitat/Range: Both open and shaded areas in foothill woodland and mixed coniferous forest.

Comments: The genus name is Greek for "glue," *kolla.* The seed coat of *Collomia* seeds becomes mucilaginous when wet. This "glue" helps keep the germinated seeds from drying out. This is a mechanism that helps store water between the first fall rains and those that may not come for several weeks later. The species name means "large-flowered."

MOUNTAIN SORREL
Oxyria digyna
Buckwheat Family (Polygonaceae)

Description: Perennial, 3–20" tall. The leaves are kidney-shaped, 1–2" wide, and occur on a long stalk. The inflorescence is an open panicle of tiny nodding flowers, with 4 petal-like sepals, 2 styles, and no petals. The flowers can also be pink, green, or yellow-green. The red fruit is flat and winged.

July–September

Habitat/Range: Rocky places in subalpine forest and the alpine zone.

Comments: The genus name is Greek for "sour," referring to the taste of the plant. The species name is Latin for "two pistils." Some Native Americans ate the stems and leaves raw and cooked. The larvae of the lustrous copper butterfly (*Lycaena cupreus*) feed on this plant.

KAREN WIESE

Mountain Sorrel

Skyrocket, Scarlet Gilia

SKYROCKET; SCARLET GILIA
Ipomopsis aggregata
Phlox Family (Polemoniaceae)

Description: Slightly hairy perennial, 12–30" tall, that often forms large colonies. The leaves are pinnately lobed and 1–2" long. The inflorescence is a 1-sided, lateral cluster of 1–7 trumpet-shaped flowers, 1" long and ¾" wide. Each 5-lobed flower has yellow mottling on the throat and the base of the corolla lobes. The showy stamens and style are exserted from the corolla.

June–September

Habitat/Range: Open areas and rocky places in mixed coniferous forest and subalpine forest.

Comments: The genus name is Greek for "to strike an appearance," referring to the flowers' showy appearance. The species name is Latin for "clustered," referring to the arrangement of flowers. Though Native Americans did not eat this plant, it still had many uses. The leaves were used to make a tea to treat children's colds and relieve stomachaches; a glue was made by boiling the entire plant, and a blue dye was extracted from the roots. This plant is visited by hummingbirds, hawkmoths, sphinx moths, beeflies, and long- and short-tongued bees. The hummingbirds extract nectar with their long tongues, the moths feed on the leaves at night, and the bees and beeflies bite holes in the base of the flower to reach the nectar.

KAREN CALLAHAN

Crimson Columbine

CRIMSON COLUMBINE

Aquilegia formosa
Buttercup Family (Ranunculaceae)

Description: Perennial, 18–42" tall. The leaves are lobed, up to 1 ½" wide, and occur on the lower half of the stem. The flowers are 1 ½" long, nodding, with 5 red, ovate, petal-like sepals. The 5 yellow and red petals are spurs that are reflexed between the sepals. The 5 bright yellow pistils and 10–18 stamens extend beyond the flower, making pollination easy. The fruit is erect, up to 1" long, and filled with small seeds.

June–August

Habitat/Range: Shaded areas in foothill woodland, mixed coniferous forest, subalpine forest, and pinyon-juniper woodland.

Comments: The origin of the genus name is uncertain. One theory is that it comes from the Latin for "eagle," referring to the spurs, which might suggest claws. Another theory is that it comes from *aquilegus,* "water-drawer," from the habitat the plant prefers. A beautiful cream-colored columbine, *Aquilegia pubescens,* occurs in rocky areas in subalpine forest and the alpine zone. Occasionally these two plants grow side by side and hybridize, producing offspring with characteristics of both. Columbines are a source of nectar for hummingbirds.

RED LARKSPUR
Delphinium nudicaule
Buttercup Family (Ranunculaceae)

Description: Perennial 6–20" tall. The leaves are lobed, 1–4" wide, and occur along the lower half of the stem. The inflorescence is a raceme of 10–25 flowers along a stem. The funnel-shaped flowers have 5 petal-like sepals and 4 tiny petals inside. The upper sepal is reflexed to form a spur.

March–June

Habitat/Range: Shaded areas and moist rocky places in foothill woodland and mixed coniferous forest.

Comments: The genus name is Latin for "dolphin," referring to the shape of the flower bud. The species name is Latin for "naked stem," referring to the absence of leaves on the upper part of the stems. All members of the genus *Delphinium* are poisonous to humans and livestock.

Red Larkspur

Wavy-Leaved Paintbrush

WAVY-LEAVED PAINTBRUSH
Castilleja applegatei
Figwort Family (Scrophulariaceae)

Description: Glandular, hairy perennial, with few stems, up to 30" tall. The leaves are lanceolate, 1–2 ½" long, with wavy margins. The inflorescence is 2–8" long with many colorful leafy bracts. The small, tubular flowers, ¾–1 ½" long, are tucked away between the bracts and the calyx, which is 1" long. Each flower has 2 lips, with the top lip beaklike and the bottom lip consisting of 3 small green teeth.

May–August

Habitat/Range: Open, especially dry areas in mixed coniferous forest, subalpine forest, and sagebrush scrub.

Comments: The genus name honors the Spanish botanist Domingo Castillejo (1744–1793). The yellow stamens and styles protrude beyond the petals, making it easy for hummingbirds to pollinate. The larvae of the leanira checkerspot butterfly (*Thessalia leanira*) feed on the leaves of members of this genus.

KAREN WIESE

Giant Red Paintbrush

GIANT RED PAINTBRUSH
Castilleja miniata
Figwort Family (Scrophulariaceae)

Description: Perennial, 12–30" tall. The leaves are lanceolate and 1–2" long. The inflorescence is a soft-hairy cluster of red bracts and the calyces, 1–6" long. The 2-lipped, tubular flowers, ½–1 ½" long, have a yellow upper lip with a red margin and a lower lip with green teeth.

May–September

Habitat/Range: Wetlands in mixed coniferous forest and subalpine forest.

Comments: The species name is Latin for "cinnabar red," referring to the color of the inflorescence. This plant is commonly parasitic on willow.

SCARLET MONKEYFLOWER
Mimulus cardinalis
Figwort Family (Scrophulariaceae)

Description: Hairy and glandular perennial, prostrate or erect, 1–3' tall. The leaves are opposite, oblong, ¾–3" long, and coarsely serrate. The flowers occur in pairs in the axils of the upper leaves. The 5-lobed, 2-lipped, tubular flowers are 1 ½–2" long, with the upper lip arched forward and the lower lip reflexed. The throat floor of the flower has yellow, hairy ridges. The contrast between the yellow and the red acts as a nectar guide that attracts pollinators.

April–October

Habitat/Range: Wetlands, stream banks, in foothill woodland and mixed coniferous forest.

Comments: *Cardinal* has over time become a synonym for *scarlet*. The original Latin meaning of *cardinalis* was "principal," and it was thus used for officials in the Roman Catholic Church. Their red robes gave the term its new meaning, and the word was transformed by botanists into a Neo-Latin species name.

KAREN WIESE

Scarlet Monkeyflower

Bush Monkeyflower; Sticky Monkeyflower

BUSH MONKEYFLOWER; STICKY MONKEYFLOWER

Mimulus aurantiacus
Figwort Family (Scrophulariaceae)

Description: Subshrub or shrub with many branches, up to 4' tall. The leaves are opposite, linear, 1–3" long, and often glandular, hence another common name, sticky monkeyflower. The flowers occur in pairs in the axils of the upper leaves. The 5-lobed, 2-lipped trumpet-shaped flowers are up to 3" long. The throat floor of the flower often has 2 broad lines of dark orange that act as nectar guides for insects.

March–August

Habitat/Range: Rocky places in foothill woodland and mixed coniferous forest.

Comments: The genus name is Latin for a "mime" or "comic actor," referring to the corolla, which looks like a grinning face. The species name is Latin for "orange-red," which refers to the corolla. The larvae of the variable checkerspot butterfly (*Euphydryas chalcedona*) feed on this plant.

Scarlet Penstemon; Beaked Penstemon

SCARLET PENSTEMON; BEAKED PENSTEMON

Penstemon rostriflorus
Figwort Family (Scrophulariaceae)

Description: Woody perennial 1–3' tall. The leaves are opposite, linear, entire, and 1–3" long. The flowers occur in pairs in the axils of the upper leaves. The 2-lipped, trumpet-shaped flowers are ¾–1" long. The upper lip forms a hood or beak over the anthers; the lower lip is 3-lobed and reflexed.

June–August

Habitat/Range: Open areas in mixed coniferous forest, subalpine forest, pinyon-juniper woodland, and sagebrush scrub.

Comments: The species name is Latin for "beaked," referring to the upper lip or beak of the corolla. The scarlet color attracts hummingbirds, which feed on the nectar and pollinate the flowers.

YELLOW FLOWERS

KAREN WIESE

This section includes flowers from a pale cream to a bright, golden yellow. Some species have two-colored flowers, such as yellow and pink or yellow and white. If the predominant color is yellow, they are included here. Many species with yellow flowers also have green or orange flower variations or turn red as they age. You may need to check those sections if the flower you are searching for is not found here.

Lomatium

LOMATIUM
Lomatium utriculatum
Carrot Family (Apiaceae)

Description: Perennial, up to 2' tall, some-times hairy. The leaves are finely dissected. The inflorescence is an umbel with 5–20 rays with clusters of small flowers at the end of each ray. The flat fruit has wings or ribs on the side margins.

February–May

Habitat/Range: Open areas in foothill wood-land, mixed coniferous forest, and sagebrush scrub.

Comments: The genus name is Greek for "a border," referring to the borders or wings on the seeds. The taproots, an important food for some Native Americans, were often dried, ground into flour, and made into cakes—hence an alternative common name, biscuitroot.

SPEAR-LEAVED AGOSERIS
Agoseris retrorsa
Aster Family (Asteraceae)

Description: Perennial 4–20" tall, covered with soft hairs when young. The woolly hairs help the young plant deter predators and re-flect excessive light. The lobes of the dande-lion-like leaves are angled downward, toward the leaf base. When broken, the leaves yield a milky sap. The inflorescence is a head of many straplike yellow ray flowers.

May–August

Habitat/Range: Open areas in foothill wood-land and mixed coniferous forest.

Comments: This species name means "bent downward," referring to the lobes of the leaves. An other common name of this plant is moun-tain dandelion, due to its resemblance to the common dandelion.

Spear-Leaved Agoseris

SOFT ARNICA
Arnica mollis
Aster Family (Asteraceae)

Description: Aromatic, glandular perennial, up to 2' tall. The leaves are opposite, oblanceolate to obovate, and occur in 3–5 pairs along the stem. Each plant has 1–3 flower heads with yellow ray and disk flowers.

July–September

Habitat/Range: Wetlands in subalpine forest.

Comments: Tinctures, oils, salves, and even just the bruised fresh plant have been used externally in Europe and by some Native Americans as a muscle liniment for bruises, sprains, strains, and arthritis. Arnica works by dilating the blood vessels and allowing more blood to the injured tissues.

Soft Arnica

Brewer's Golden Aster

BREWER'S GOLDEN ASTER
Aster breweri
Aster Family (Asteraceae)

Description: Perennial, single-stemmed herb or multistemmed shrub from a woody base, up to 3' tall. The leaves are lanceolate to ovate, occur along the stem, and can be entire or serrate and from smooth to hairy. The flower heads are atypical for an aster, for there are only disk flowers. The flower heads are bell shaped and are up to ¾" long.

July–September

Habitat/Range: Open and semishaded areas in mixed coniferous forest, subalpine forest, and pinyon-juniper woodland.

Arrow-Leaved Balsamroot

ARROW-LEAVED BALSAMROOT
Balsamorhiza sagittata
Aster Family (Asteraceae)

Description: Aromatic, hairy perennial, with several erect stems up to 30" tall. The leaves are triangular, mostly basal, and up to 19" long. The base of each leaf blade has 2 lobes that make the leaves resemble an arrowhead. The saucer-shaped flowers are 2–4" in diameter with yellow ray and disk flowers.

May–July

Habitat/Range: Open areas in mixed conifer forest, sagebrush scrub, and pinyon-juniper woodland.

Comments: The genus name is Greek for "glandular root," referring to the glandular sap of the taproot. The species name is Latin for "arrow," referring to the shape of the leaf. Some Native Americans made a chewing gum and a topical antiseptic for minor wounds out of the resin. The thick roots were a highly prized food of Native Americans.

RABBITBRUSH
Chrysothamnus nauseosus
Aster Family (Asteraceae)

Description: Aromatic shrub up to 6' tall, with several branched stems. The leaves are linear, up to 3" long, and occur regularly along the stem. The inflorescence is a dense cluster of flower heads, each with a few small disk flowers.

August–October

Habitat/Range: Open areas in mixed coniferous forest, pinyon-juniper woodland, and sagebrush scrub.

Comments: The genus name is Greek for "golden shrub," referring to the color of the profuse flowers. The species name is Latin for "nauseous," referring to the odor of the crushed leaves. Some Native Americans used the flowers to produce yellow and orange dyes and the inner bark to produce a green dye.

Rabbitbrush

WHITE-STEMMED GOLDENBUSH

Ericameria discoidea
Aster Family (Asteraceae)

Description: Resinous, compact shrub up to 2' tall, with stems covered with white feltlike hairs. The numerous leaves are threadlike, 2" long, and occur along the stem. The inflorescence is a cluster of numerous disk flowers that are ½" long, yellow, and have a pungent odor.

July–October

Habitat/Range: Open and rocky areas in subalpine forest, pinyon-juniper woodland, and the alpine zone.

White-Stemmed Goldenbush

KAREN WIESE

KAREN WIESE

Woolly Sunflower

WOOLLY SUNFLOWER

Eriophyllum lanatum
Aster Family (Asteraceae)

Description: White woolly annual, perennial, or subshrub, with several varieties throughout the Sierra Nevada. This multistemmed plant grows up to 3' tall. The leaves are alternate, entire to lobed, and up to 3" long. The saucer-shaped flower heads are less than 1" wide, with yellow ray and disk flowers.

April–August

Habitat/Range: Open and rocky places in foothill woodland, mixed coniferous forest, and subalpine forest.

Comments: The genus name is Greek for "woolly leaf," referring to the fuzz on the leaves of most species in this genus. The species name, Latin for "wool," reiterates the point, for the entire plant is covered with a dense mat of fine white hairs.

KAREN WIESE

Bigelow's Sneezeweed

BIGELOW'S SNEEZEWEED
Helenium bigelovii
Aster Family (Asteraceae)

Description: Perennial 1–4' tall. The basal leaves are oblanceolate, entire, and up to 9" long. The stem leaves often clasp the stem or continue down as thin wings. Each plant has 1 to several flower heads. The flowers heads are a sphere of disk flowers surrounded by a fringe of ray flowers, often pointing down. The disk flowers can be yellow or reddish purple; the ray flowers are yellow and almost 1" long.

June–August

Habitat/Range: Wetlands, especially meadows, in foothill woodland, mixed coniferous forest, and subalpine forest.

Comments: Linnaeus named this genus after Helen of Troy, who, according to Homeric legend, was the daughter of Zeus and whose abduction led to the Trojan War.

SHAGGY HAWKWEED
Hieracium horridum
Aster Family (Asteraceae)

Description: Densely hairy perennial with milky sap and 1 to several branched stems up to 1' tall. The leaves occur along the stem and are oblong and up to 4" long. The inflorescence is a cluster of 6–15 flower heads; each flower is about ⅜" long. Each flower head has only ray flowers.

July–August

Habitat/Range: Rocky places in mixed coniferous forest, subalpine forest, and the alpine zone.

Comments: The genus name is Greek for "hawk," referring to the ancient belief that hawks would eat these plants to sharpen their eyesight. The species name means "bristly" or "prickly."

KAREN WIESE

Shaggy Hawkweed

ALPINE GOLD
Hulsea algida
Aster Family (Asteraceae)

Description: Hairy perennial, up to 16" tall. The leaves are glandular, alternate, coarsely serrate, and up to 4" long, occurring at the base of the plant. Each plant has 1–2 flower heads that are 2 ½" wide, with both ray and disk flowers.

July–August

Habitat/Range: Rocky places in the alpine zone.

Comments: The genus name honors the U.S. Army surgeon and botanist Gilbert Hulse (1807–1883). The species name is Latin for "cold," describing its preferred climate. Bighorn sheep eat all parts of this plant, including the roots.

Alpine Gold

Common Tarweed

COMMON TARWEED
Madia elegans
Aster Family (Asteraceae)

Description: Aromatic annual, up to 3' tall. The leaves are linear, soft-hairy, and glandular, up to 8" long. The saucer-shaped flower heads have both ray and disk flowers and are up to 2" wide. The ray flowers have 2 notches at the end of each petal and may have a maroon dot at the base.

May–August

Habitat/Range: Open areas in foothill woodland and mixed coniferous forest.

Comments: The flower heads of this plant will close at midday in the hot sun to protect their pollen, then reopen in the late afternoon. The glandular resin in the plant gives the plant its other common name, tarweed. The rich, oily seeds were gathered by some Native Americans in midsummer and used to make a thin mush.

KAREN WIESE

Pyrrocoma

PYRROCOMA
Pyrrocoma apargiodes
Aster Family (Asteraceae)

Description: Perennial, up to 7" tall. The basal leaves are lanceolate, leathery, and coarsely serrate. The stem leaves are smaller and generally entire. The flower head has both ray and disk flowers and occurs on a flower stalk, with usually 1 flower per plant. The flower head is about ¾" long.

July–September

Habitat/Range: Open areas and rocky places, including meadows, in subalpine forest and the alpine zone.

SILKY RAILLARDELLA
Raillardella argentea
Aster Family (Asteraceae)

Description: Hairy perennial, up to 6" tall. The leaves are oblanceolate, 3" long, and appear silvery because they are covered with soft hairs. The inflorescence is a solitary flower head on a leafless stem. The flower heads have only disk flowers.

July–August

Habitat/Range: Open areas and rocky places in subalpine forest and the alpine zone.

Comments: The species name is Latin for "silvery," referring to the appearance of the plant due to the hairs.

KAREN WIESE

Silky Raillardella

CALIFORNIA CONEFLOWER
Rudbeckia californica
Aster Family (Asteraceae)

Description: Tall, unbranched perennial, 2–6' tall. The leaves, 4–12" long, are lanceolate to ovate. The flower heads have both ray and disk flowers and are 4–6" across. The ray flowers, 1–2" long, are yellow, drooping, and located at the base of a large cone. This distinctive cone is composed of numerous disk flowers and stands 1–2" high.

June–August

Habitat/Range: Wetlands in mixed coniferous forest.

Comments: The genus name honors the Swedish father and son who were professors of botany and predecessors of Linnaeus, O. J. Rudbeck (1630–1702) and O.O. Rudbeck (1660–1740). Some Native Americans cooked the entire flower bud for food and collected the ripe seeds in the fall to grind for meal.

California Coneflower

ARROWHEAD BUTTERWEED
Senecio triangularis
Aster Family (Asteraceae)

Description: Perennial, 18–48" tall. This plant is distinguished by the triangular leaves, 2–8" long, alternately arranged along the stem. The inflorescence is a cluster of 30 or more yellow flower heads, 1 ¼" wide, having both ray and disk flowers.

July–September

Habitat/Range: Wetlands in mixed coniferous forest and subalpine forest.

Comments: The common name "butterweed" comes from its yellow color. The genus name is Latin for "old man," referring to the white pappus of the fruit, which looks like a white-haired man's head. The species name is Latin for "triangular," referring to the leaves. Members of the genus *Senecio* have also been called "groundsel," which is derived from an Anglo-Saxon word meaning "ground-swallower," because some species are common weeds.

Arrowhead Butterweed

KAREN WIESE

Northern Goldenrod

NORTHERN GOLDENROD
Solidago multiradiata
Aster Family (Asteraceae)

Description: Perennial up to 18" tall. The leaves are linear, smaller toward the top of the plant. The inflorescence is a cluster of a few to many flower heads. Each flower head is less than ½" wide, with yellow ray and disk flowers.

June–September

Habitat/Range: Open areas and rocky places in subalpine forest and the alpine zone.

Comments: The genus name is Latin for "solid," alluding to the purported medicinal value of the plant. Some Native Americans of the Sierra Nevada used the crushed fresh leaves to treat wounds.

LEMMON'S DRABA
Draba lemmonii var. *lemmonii*
Mustard Family (Brassicaceae)

Description: Hairy, mat-forming perennial, up to 6" tall. The leaves are basal, obovate, and less than 1" long. There are up to 30 small, 4-petaled flowers clustered on top of a flower stalk. The fruit can be up to ½" long and is ascending and twisted.

July–August

Habitat/Range: Rocky places in subalpine forest and the alpine zone.

Comments: The genus name is Greek for "acrid," referring to the bitter taste of some members of this family. The species name honors John G. Lemmon (1832–1908), who with his wife, Sara Plummer Lemmon, collected plants throughout the West.

KAREN WIESE

Lemmon's Draba

Cushion Stenotus

CUSHION STENOTUS
Stenotus acaulis
Aster Family (Asteraceae)

Description: Mat-forming perennial up to 20" wide and 2–4" tall, with many branches from a woody base. The leaves are crowded, oblanceolate, and less than 4" long. The inflorescence is a solitary flower head, with many on each plant. Each flower head is approximately 1" wide with both ray and disk flowers.

May–August

Habitat/Range: Open areas and rocky places in mixed coniferous forest, subalpine forest, sagebrush scrub, and the alpine zone.

Comments: The species name is Latin for "stemless," referring to the seeming lack of stems.

KAREN WIESE

Mountain Mule Ears

MOUNTAIN MULE EARS
Wyethia mollis
Aster Family (Asteraceae)

Description: Perennial, 1–2' tall. The leaves are oblanceolate, 8–16" long, and occur mostly at the base of the plant. The young leaves are covered with silver hairs that reflect intense sunlight. There are 1 to few flower heads per plant, up to 3" wide. Each flower head has large yellow ray flowers surrounding yellow disk flowers.

May–August

Habitat/Range: Open areas and rocky places in mixed coniferous forest, subalpine forest, and sagebrush scrub.

Comments: The genus name honors Nathaniel J. Wyeth (1802–1856), an explorer who sent floral specimens from the Northwest to the Harvard botanist Thomas Nuttall. Nuttall named this plant after Wyeth. The species name is Latin for "soft-hairy," referring to the leaves. The common name comes from the shape of the woolly leaves. Some Native Americans used the roots as a medicine for sores, burns, and rheumatism, preparing the roots by baking them in hot ashes and applying it as a poultice, or by drying and grinding them and applying it as a salve.

WESTERN WALLFLOWER

Erysimum capitatum
Mustard Family (Brassicaceae)

Description: Biennial or short-lived perennial, up to 3' tall. The leaves are linear to spoon-shaped, smooth edged or serrate, and up to 10" long. The 4-petaled flowers are ¾" wide and clustered at the top of the plant. The fruit is narrow, ascending, and 1–6" long.

March–July

Habitat/Range: Open areas in all plant communities.

Comments: The genus name is derived from the Greek word for "to help" or "to save," referring to the purported medicinal value of some species.

KAREN WIESE

Western Wallflower

PACIFIC STONECROP

Sedum spathulifolium
Stonecrop Family (Crassulaceae)

Description: Succulent perennial, up to 9" tall, with a basal rosette of leaves 2 ½" in diameter. The leaves are less than 1" long with a rounded tip. The inflorescence is a flat-topped cluster of 8–60 small star-shaped flowers.

May–July

Habitat/Range: Rocky areas in foothill woodland and mixed coniferous forest.

Comments: The species name means "spatulate-leaved."

RICHARD HANES

Pacific Stonecrop

RICHARD HANES

Narrow-Leaved Lotus

NARROW-LEAVED LOTUS
Lotus oblongifolius
Pea Family (Fabaceae)

Description: Sprawling or ascending, often hairy perennial, 8–20" tall. The leaves have 3–11 elliptic, paired leaflets. The inflorescence is an umbel of 2–6 flowers. The pea-family flowers are up to ½" long. The flowers have a yellow banner and white keel. The fruits are narrow and 1" long.

May–August

Habitat/Range: Open areas and wetlands in mixed coniferous forest, pinyon-juniper woodland, and sagebrush scrub.

Comments: When a bee lands on the wings of this plant, its weight pulls the petals down and the keel splits open, exposing the stamens, which are loaded with pollen. The stamens dust the bees with pollen, and the keel springs back after the bee leaves. When mature, the seeds of this plant are forcibly expelled many feet when the mature fruit twists and unzips.

Tinker's Penny

TINKER'S PENNY
Hypericum anagalloides
St. John's Wort Family (Hypericaceae)

Description: Annual or perennial that forms a small, branching mat, 1–10" wide. The leaves are linear, ½" long, opposite, and have clear or green glands that secrete a red, medicinally active compound called hypericin. There are usually 1–7 flowers per stem, each ½" wide and saucer-shaped. The flowers have 5 petals that alternate with 5 sepals, and 15–25 stamens.

June–August

Habitat/Range: Wetlands in mixed coniferous forest and subalpine forest.

Comments: The common name refers to the small, round flower, which gives the impression of a penny. The Sierra Nevada Maidu treated wounds and venereal diseases with this plant.

KAREN WIESE

STEVE MATSON

St. John's Wort

ST. JOHN'S WORT
Hypericum formosum var. *scouleri*
St. John's Wort Family (Hypericaceae)

Description: Erect perennial, 8–28" tall. The leaves are ovate, opposite, ½–1" long, and have black dots along the margins. The inflorescence is a cyme, with 3–25 flowers per stem. Each flower has 5 sepals and 5 oblong petals, both black-dotted. The flowers are 1" wide. The numerous stamens are in bundles.

June–September

Habitat/Range: Wetlands in foothill woodland and mixed coniferous forest.

Comments: The genus name is Greek for "above an icon," referring to the act of placing St. John's Wort sprigs above religious images to drive off evil spirits. The common name refers to the fact that in Europe, the plant flowers around June 24, the day that honors John the Baptist and is the time of the summer solstice. It was used in solstice rites and rituals by the Druids, Celts, and Saxons. The species name is Latin for "beautiful." The variety name honors Dr. John Scouler, a Scottish physician and naturalist who explored the Columbia River area in 1825. Touted in our times for its medicinal qualities as an anti-inflammatory, antimicrobial, diuretic, and treatment for depression, this plant has the same constituents as its nonnative, commercially cultivated relative, Klamath weed (*Hypericum perforatum*), but about half the strength.

HARTWEG'S IRIS

Iris hartwegii
Iris Family (Iridaceae)

Description: Perennial, up to 1' tall from a small rhizome. The leaves are lanceolate and up to 1 ½" long. The inflorescence has 1–3 flowers. The 3 petal-like sepals are reflexed downward, acting as a landing pad for insects. The 3 petals are erect. Each sepal has a stamen that is located just beneath a petal-like, V-notched style. When an insect lands on a sepal, it crawls into the center of the plant toward the nectar, distributing pollen as it brushes against the style while picking up a new load of pollen.

March–July

Habitat/Range: Shaded, especially dry areas in foothill woodland and mixed coniferous forest.

Comments: The species name honors the German botanist Karl Theodor Hartweg (1812–1871), who collected in the Sierra Nevada foothills in 1846 for the Horticultural Society in London.

Hartweg's Iris

KAREN WIESE

KAREN CALLAHAN

Yellow Star Tulip; Pussy Ears

YELLOW STAR TULIP; PUSSY EARS

Calochortus monophyllus
Lily Family (Liliaceae)

Description: Perennial, up to 8" from a bulb. Each plant has 1 basal leaf, 6" long. The inflorescence ranges from a solitary flower to a cluster of up to 6 flowers. Each flower is bell-shaped, with 3 sepals and 3 petals. The inside of the corolla is densely hairy. The erect, linear fruit is ¾" long.

May–July

Habitat/Range: Shaded areas in foothill woodland and mixed coniferous forest.

Comments: The genus name is Greek for "beautiful grass," although this plant is not really a true grass. The species name is Latin for "one-leaved." Some Native Americans harvested the bulbs in late spring and ate them raw, cooked, or ground into meal.

Pretty Face

PRETTY FACE
Triteleia ixioides
Lily Family (Liliaceae)

Description: Perennial, from a corm, up to 30" tall but usually shorter. The 2–3 leaves are basal, up to 1' long, lanceolate, and often wither by the time the flower blooms. The inflorescence is an umbel of trumpet-shaped flowers. Each flower has 3 petal-like sepals and 3 petals, with a purple stripe in the middle of each perianth part. The purple stripe acts as a nectar guide for insects.

May–July

Habitat/Range: Open or shaded areas in foothill woodland and mixed coniferous forest.

Comments: The genus name is Latin for "three," referring to the triads of sepals and petals.

BLAZING STAR
Mentzelia laevicaulis
Loasa Family (Loasaceae)

Description: Stout, hairy perennial, up to 3' tall. The leaves are oblanceolate, lobed, and vary from 9" long at the base to 4" long on the stem. The 1–3 star-shaped flowers occur in clusters on each plant. Each flower is 4–6" wide, has 5 lanceolate petals, and many stamens.

June–October

Habitat/Range: Open areas, especially rocky and sandy places in foothill woodland, mixed coniferous forest, pinyon-juniper woodland, and sagebrush scrub.

Comments: The genus name honors the German botanist Christian Mentzel (1622–1701). The numerous stamens and the star-shaped corolla suggest a "blazing star." From the leaves, some Native Americans made a tea for stomachaches and a topical medicine for skin diseases.

Blazing Star

Yellow Pond-Lily

KAREN CALLAHAN

YELLOW POND-LILY
Nuphar lutea ssp. *polysepala*
Water-Lily Family (Nymphaeaceae)

Description: Aquatic perennial, often occurring in colonies. The leaves are heart shaped, 16" wide, and float. The inflorescence is a solitary flower, 2–3" wide. The flower has 5–14 ovate, petal-like sepals; the 10–20 petals are often red-tinged. The stigma is ¾" wide and disklike.

May–September

Habitat/Range: Wetlands, especially ponds and slow streams, in foothill woodland and mixed coniferous forest.

Comments: The genus name is the Arabic name of this plant. The species name is Latin for "yellow," referring to the flower. This plant was a food source for Native Americans throughout the West, who harvested the seeds in midsummer to fall and put them in a hole to ferment. Weeks later, the best seeds were collected, dried, and roasted. The seeds were then ground and made into a flour for bread or cereal. The seeds would also be popped like popcorn and eaten. The roots were dug up and dried and ground into flour or cooked in soups and stews.

Woody-Fruited Evening Primrose

WOODY-FRUITED EVENING PRIMROSE
Oenothera xylocarpa
Evening-Primrose Family (Onagraceae)

Description: Gray-green perennial in a rosette. The leaves are prostrate, have purple splotches, and are round to oblanceolate with several small lobes at the base. The large flowers occur in the axils of the leaves. The saucer-shaped flowers have 4 petals, 4 reflexed sepals, and a 4-lobed stigma. The fruit is a curved, wrinkled cylinder, up to 3 ½" long.

July–August

Habitat/Range: Open areas, especially gravelly places, in mixed coniferous forest and subalpine forest.

Comments: The flowers open at dusk and remain open throughout the night for evening pollinating moths. The short-lived flowers close the next day and the petals turn deep red.

LOBB'S BUCKWHEAT
Eriogonum lobbii var. *lobbii*
Buckwheat Family (Polygonaceae)

Description: Woolly, sprawling perennial, from a thick, woody stem, 6" tall and 2–16" wide. The leaves are soft-hairy, round, up to 1 ½" wide, and basal. The inflorescence is an umbel of 1 to several spheres of densely clustered flowers, 2" wide, on a long, prostrate stem, 2–8" long. Instead of petals, each flower has 6 small, petal-like sepals. The flowers turn red-orange with age.

June–August

Habitat/Range: Rocky places in mixed coniferous forest, subalpine forest, and the alpine zone.

Comments: The genus name is Greek for "wool knee," referring to the hairy nodes of many species, including this one. Some Native Americans used the seeds of buckwheat to make a flour. Birds, small mammals, and deer depend on the seeds of this genus for food.

Lobb's Buckwheat

Sulfur Flower; Sulfur Buckwheat

KAREN VJIESE

SULFUR FLOWER; SULFUR BUCKWHEAT

Eriogonum umbellatum
Buckwheat Family (Polygonaceae)

Description: White, woolly perennial to shrub, up to 2' tall. The leaves are elliptic, occur at the base of a thick woody stem, and are especially woolly beneath. The inflorescence is a cluster of flowers on an umbel of 5–10 rays. Instead of petals, each flower has petal-like sepals. The bright yellow flowers turn orange with age.

May–September

Habitat/Range: Open areas and rocky places in mixed coniferous forest, subalpine forest, pinyon-juniper woodland, sagebrush scrub, and the alpine zone.

Comments: The genus name is Greek for "wool knee," referring to the hairy nodes of many species. The species name is Latin for "umbrella-shaped," referring to the arrangement of the flowers. The common name refers to the bright sulfur-colored flowers. Some Native Americans used the leaves to make a tea for colic and headaches, the roots to make a tea for colds, and the flowers to make an eye wash.

KAREN WIESE

Alpine Buttercup

ALPINE BUTTERCUP
Ranunculus eschscholtzii
Buttercup Family (Ranunculaceae)

Description: Perennial, up to 10" tall. The leaves are round to kidney-shaped, 3-lobed, and occur at the base of the plant and on the lower stem. The saucer-shaped flowers, 1" wide, occur at the end of a stem that rises above the leaves.

July–August

Habitat/Range: Wetlands and rocky places in mixed coniferous forest, subalpine forest, and the alpine zone.

Comments: The species name honors the Russian surgeon and naturalist Johann Friedrich Gustav von Eschscholtz (1793–1831), who in 1815 was sent by his government on a scientific exploration of the Pacific Coast.

WESTERN BUTTERCUP
Ranunculus occidentalis
Buttercup Family (Ranunculaceae)

Description: One of 20 species of *Ranunculus* in the Sierra Nevada, this common buttercup is a perennial, up to 2' tall. The leaves are soft-hairy, ovate in outline, lobed, and basal. The saucer-shaped flowers, ¾" wide, have 5–6 very shiny petals.

May–July

Habitat/Range: Moist places such as meadows in foothill woodland and coniferous forest.

Comments: The genus name comes from the name given the plant by the Roman naturalist Pliny (A.D. 23–79); it means "little frog," referring to the wet habitats inhabited by both frogs and buttercups. The seeds of the buttercup were an important food for some Native Californians. Before being consumed, the seeds were lightly roasted with hot coals in flat baskets to remove their bitter taste.

KAREN WIESE

Western Buttercup

JOESPH MEDEIROS

Club-Moss Ivesia

CLUB-MOSS IVESIA
Ivesia lycopodioides
Rose Family (Rosaceae)

Description: Perennial with erect and sprawling stems, 1–12" long. The leaves are ½–6" long, compound, with as many as 70 leaflets per leaf! The overall shape of the leaves is cylindrical, with most of the leaves occurring at the base of the plant. The inflorescence is a headlike cluster of up to 15 saucer-shaped flowers. Each flower has 5 sepals, 5 petals, and many pistils, all typical characteristics of flowers in the rose family.

July–August

Habitat/Range: Rocky places, especially meadows, in subalpine forest and the alpine zone.

Comments: The genus name honors Lieutenant Eli Ives (1779–1861), leader of a Pacific Railroad Survey and Yale University pharmacologist. The species name is Latin for "like a club moss," referring to the leaves' resemblance to a club moss. A club moss isn't a moss. It is a primitive, non-flowering, vascular plant more closely related to a fern.

EDWARD RINGROSE

Shrubby Cinquefoil

SHRUBBY CINQUEFOIL
Potentilla fruiticosa
Rose Family (Rosaceae)

Description: Multibranched shrub, up to 3' tall. The leaves are pinnate, with 2–3 pairs of linear leaflets. The saucer-shaped 5-petaled flowers occur at the end of the twigs.

June–August

Habitat/Range: Open, especially moist areas in subalpine forest and the alpine zone.

Comments: The genus name is Latin for "powerful," referring to the plant's reputed medicinal value.

STICKY CINQUEFOIL
Potentilla glandulosa
Rose Family (Rosaceae)

Description: Glandular, hairy perennial, up to 30" tall. The leaves are pinnately compound, basal, with 3–5 pairs of leaflets per leaf. Each of the leaflets is ovate in outline and serrate. The inflorescence is a cyme of 2–30 saucer-shaped flowers. The flowers can be light yellow or white.

May–July

Habitat/Range: Open areas in foothill woodland, mixed coniferous forest, and subalpine forest.

Comments: The genus name is Latin for "powerful," referring to the plant's reputed medicinal value. The species name means "glandular." Some Native Americans made a lotion from the stems and leaves for an astringent and used the leaves in a tea to treat headaches and stomachaches.

KAREN CALLAHAN

Sticky Cinquefoil

Antelope Bush; Bitterbrush

KAREN WIESE

ANTELOPE BUSH; BITTERBRUSH
Purshia tridentata
Rose Family (Rosaceae)

Description: Many-branched shrub, up to 16' tall but mostly smaller. The leaves are wedge shaped, 3-toothed, and rolled under. The inflorescence is a solitary, 5-petaled, funnel-shaped flower, ¾" wide on the side branches. The flowers have approximately 25 stamens.

May–July

Habitat/Range: Open areas in mixed coniferous forest, pinyon-juniper woodland, and sagebrush scrub.

Comments: The genus name honors the author of an early North American flora Frederick T. Pursh (1774–1820), who received the plant collections from the Lewis and Clark Expedition. The species name is Latin for "three-toothed," referring to the leaves. Some Native Americans obtained a violet dye from the cooked, ripe seed coats. Although this shrub tastes bitter, it is a nutritious and important food source for deer, especially in the winter on windswept, snow-free slopes. The larvae of the Behr's hairstreak butterfly (*Satyrium behrii*) feed on the plant.

Alpine Paintbrush

ALPINE PAINTBRUSH
Castilleja nana
Figwort Family (Scrophulariaceae)

Description: Hairy perennial, 2–10" tall. The leaves are linear, ⅜–1 ⅜" long, and often 3-lobed. The inflorescence is a spike, 1–5" long, of subtly colored bracts and calyces. The 2-lipped, tubular flowers are ½–¾" long and nestled in the bracts. The upper lip is pale yellow, often with purple spots and occasionally with black tips.

July–August

Habitat/Range: Open areas and rocky places in subalpine forest and the alpine zone.

Comments: The genus name honors the Spanish botanist Domingo Castillejo (1744–1793). The species name is Latin for "dwarf."

PINE-WOODS LOUSEWORT
Pedicularis semibarbata
Figwort Family (Scrophulariaceae)

Description: Slightly hairy perennial, 4" tall, with an extensive underground stem. The leaves are finely lobed and fernlike, basal, and 2–7" long. The small, tubular flowers are hidden beneath the leaves in the center of the plant, close to the ground. The flowers are up to 1" long and have a hairy, hooded upper lip, which is often tinged purple or red, and a 3-lobed lower lip.

May–July

Habitat/Range: Open areas in coniferous forest and subalpine forest.

Comments: The genus name is Latin for "louse," a reference to an old belief that livestock that ate members of this genus would get lice. The common name, "lousewort," also refers to this belief; wort means "plant" in Middle English.

Pine-Woods Lousewort

Seep-Spring Monkeyflower

SEEP-SPRING MONKEYFLOWER
Mimulus guttatus
Figwort Family (Scrophulariaceae)

Description: Annual or rhizomed perennial, up to 5' tall but usually shorter. The leaves are oval, opposite, and up to 3" long. The inflorescence is a raceme of at least 5 tubular flowers. The 5-lobed, 2-lipped flowers are up to 1 ½" long, with the upper lip curved upward and the lower lip with 3 reflexed lobes. The throat floor and lower lobes of the corolla often have red freckles that attract pollinators and act nectar guides.

March–August

Habitat/Range: Wetlands in foothill woodland, mixed coniferous forest, and subalpine forest.

Comments: The species name is Latin for "spotted throat," referring to the freckles on the corolla. Some Native Americans ate the leaves and stems of this plant as salad greens. The larvae of the common buckeye butterfly (*Junonia coenia*) feed on this plant.

KAREN CALLAHAN

Mountain Violet

MOUNTAIN VIOLET
Viola purpurea
Violet Family (Violaceae)

Description: Hairy perennial, up to 4" tall. The leaves are ovate, up to 2" long, and on a leaf stalk up to 6" long that originates at the base of the plant. The underside of the leaves is often purple. The nodding, funnel-shaped flowers are 5/8" long and have 5 petals. The 2 uppermost petals are purple on the outside. The 3 lower petals are joined into a spur and have purple nectar guides that attract insects to the nectar glands inside the spur. The side petals have tiny hairs that brush the pollen off the pollinators.

April–June

Habitat/Range: Open areas in mixed coniferous forest, subalpine forest, and sagebrush scrub.

Comments: The species name is Latin for "purple," referring to the purple on the undersides of the leaves and backs of the upper petals. In addition to having flowers that are moth and bee pollinated, this plant has cleistogamous flowers that are budlike and self-pollinating. These flowers ensure that seeds will be produced if pollinators are not present. The stems and leaves are edible when cooked.

WHITE FLOWERS

KAREN VAESE

*This section is for pure white flowers, although
many white flowers vary from white to very pale
green or very pale yellow. Other white flowers fade
to pink, red, yellow, or orange as they age.
If you cannot find the flower you are looking for
here, you may want to check those sections,
including the green section.*

Sierra Angelica

SIERRA ANGELICA
Angelica lineariloba
Carrot Family (Apiaceae)

Description: Perennial 6–54" tall. The leaves are alternate, pinnate, triangular in outline, and up to 14" long with linear leaflets. The inflorescence is an umbel of 20–40 rays each with a cluster of small flowers. The plant has small oblong fruits.

June–August

Habitat/Range: Open, rocky places in mixed coniferous forest, subalpine forest, and sagebrush scrub.

Comments: The common and scientific names are Latin for "angelic," referring to the medicinal properties of the plant, which are said to have been revealed to a monk by an angel, who told him it was a cure for the plague. The species name means "linear-lobed," referring to the leaves. This plant was prized by California Native Americans for its ability to "cure-all."

WATER HEMLOCK
Cicuta douglasii
Carrot Family (Apiaceae)

Description: Perennial 4–9' tall. The leaves are pinnate and up to 18" long. Each lanceolate leaflet is serrate, 1–4" long. The inflorescence is an umbel of 15–30 rays with small flowers.

May–September

Habitat/Range: Wetlands in foothill woodland and mixed coniferous forest.

Comments: The genus is the ancient Latin name for poisonous hemlock. Water hemlock is one of the most lethally toxic plants in North America. The toxin in the plant is called cicutoxin, a virulent poison that kills humans and livestock.

Water Hemlock

Cow Parsnip

COW PARSNIP
Heracleum lanatum
Carrot Family (Apiaceae)

Description: Finely hairy perennial 3–10' tall. The leaves are large, round in outline, and appear lobed, but they are compound with leaflets with serrate margins. Each leaf is up to 20" across. The inflorescence is a large umbel of 15–30 rays, each ray with clusters of flowers having small, obovate, often 2-notched petals. The umbel of flowers can be 5–12" across. The flat, obovate fruits are less than ½" long with 4 prominent black lines.

April–July

Habitat/Range: Moist, shaded areas in foothill woodland and mixed coniferous forest.

Comments: The genus name refers to Hercules, hero of Greek mythology, who was reported to have been the first to use the plant as medicine; the name likely came about because of the large stature of the plant. Some Native Americans ate the cooked young shoots, and they dried and ground the older stems for seasoning. The larvae of the anise swallowtail butterfly (*Papilio zelicaon*) feed on this plant.

KAREN CALLAHAN

Mountain Sweet-Cicely

MOUNTAIN SWEET-CICELY
Osmorhiza chilensis
Carrot Family (Apiaceae)

Description: Slender, finely hairy perennial, 1–4' tall. The leaves are compound, with leaflets that are serrate, ovate, and up to 3" long. The inflorescence is an umbel of 3–8 rays with a cluster of small flowers at the end of each ray. The fruits are upright and linear, less than 1" long.

May–July

Habitat/Range: Open areas in foothill woodland and mixed coniferous forest.

Comments: The genus name is Greek for "sweet root." The species name indicates that this plant is also found in Chile. The roots are aromatic, similar to anise, and used as a flavoring in drinks. The leaves are edible.

SIERRA YAMPAH
Perideridia parishii ssp. *latifolia*
Carrot Family (Apiaceae)

Description: A slender plant, up to 30" tall, from 1 or more tubers, and often growing in large colonies. The compound leaves are ovate in outline, up to 6" long with linear leaflets. The inflorescence is an umbel of 5–20 rays, each with a cluster of small white flowers.

June–September

Habitat/Range: Open areas and wetlands in foothill woodland, mixed coniferous forest, subalpine forest, and the alpine zone.

Comments: The common name is the Shoshone Indian name for this plant. The sweet-tasting tuberous roots were an important food of Native Americans, who cooked them in a firepit, ate them raw, or dried and ground them into flour. The edible leaves were consumed, and the seeds, which are similar to those of the closely related caraway, were used as a seasoning by some Native Americans.

KAREN WIESE

Sierra Yampah

RANGER'S BUTTONS
Sphenosciadium capitellatum
Carrot Family (Apiaceae)

Description: Perennial up to 6' tall, generally branched and leafy. The oblong leaf blade is 4–16" long with sparsely serrate, lanceolate leaflets. The inflorescence is a hairy umbel of 4–18 rays, each topped with a cluster of flowers that are ½" wide and together resemble spheres or buttons. The young flower heads can be purple.

July–August

Habitat/Range: Wetlands in mixed coniferous forest and subalpine forest.

Comments: The genus name is Greek for "wedge umbrella," referring to the shape of the inflorescence. The species name is Greek for "small-headed," referring to the flower heads. This plant is toxic to humans and livestock.

KAREN WIESE

Ranger's Buttons

KAREN CALLAHAN

Yarrow

YARROW
Achillea millefolium
Aster Family (Asteraceae)

Description: Strongly scented perennial up to 3' tall. The finely dissected, fernlike leaves are 2–4" long. The flower heads occur in clusters of 10–20 flowers per cluster and form a flat-topped inflorescence. Each small flower is about ½" wide.

April–August

Habitat/Range: Dry, open, and rocky places throughout the Sierra Nevada.

Comments: The genus name is purported to be derived from Achilles, hero of Homer's *Iliad*, who packed it on his comrades' wounds to stop bleeding during the Trojan War. Some Native Americans made a tea out of the leaves and flowers for a general tonic and used the crushed leaves as a dressing for wounds. The larvae of the painted lady butterfly (*Vanessa cardui*) feed on this plant.

KAREN CALLAHAN

Trail Plant

TRAIL PLANT
Adenocaulon bicolor
Aster Family (Asteraceae)

Description: Openly branched perennial 1–3' tall. The leaves are triangular, basal, 1–10" long, and cobwebby white on the underside. The few, white flower heads have both disk and ray flowers.

June–August

Habitat/Range: Shaded areas in foothill woodland and mixed coniferous forest.

Comments: The species name is Latin for "two-colored," referring to the leaves, which are dark green on the top and white on the undersides. As you brush against these as you walk, the disturbance causes the white undersides of the leaves to be exposed, marking your trail—hence the common name.

PEARLY EVERLASTING
Anaphalis margaritacea
Aster Family (Asteraceae)

Description: Erect, white, woolly perennial, 45" tall. The leaves are simple, 1–3" long, linear to lanceolate, and alternate along the stem; the basal leaves die back. The inflorescence is a cluster of flower heads less than ½" wide with pearly white bracts surrounding small, often inconspicuous flowers. The foliage and flowers of this plant often smell like maple syrup or curry.

June–August

Habitat/Range: Open areas in foothill woodland, mixed coniferous, and subalpine forest.

Comments: The genus name is Greek for "some everlasting," referring to the flower bracts, which retain their color and shape. The species is Latin for "pearl," describing the buds. Some Native Americans used the leaves as a general antiseptic and also chewed them to treat mouth ulcers. The larvae of the American lady butterfly (*Vanessa virginiensis*) and the painted lady butterfly (*Vanessa cardui*) feed on this plant.

KAREN CALLAHAN

Pearly Everlasting

PUSSYTOES
Antennaria rosea
Aster Family (Asteraceae)

Description: Perennial, forming low-growing mats, 3–16" tall. The spoon- to wedge-shaped basal leaves each have a single vein and are woolly. The inflorescence is a cluster of 3–15 flower heads, less than ⅜" wide, with rose-tinged papery bracts surrounding small, inconspicuous flowers.

June–August

Habitat/Range: Open areas and rocky places in mixed coniferous forest, subalpine forest, and the alpine zone.

Comments: The genus name is Latin for "antenna," referring to the pappus (the bristles attached to the seeds) in the male flowers, which resemble insect antennae. The common name refers to the flower heads, which resemble the toes of a feline.

Pussytoes

Dusty Maidens; Pincushion Plant

DUSTY MAIDENS; PINCUSHION PLANT
Chaenactis douglasii
Aster Family (Asteraceae)

Description: Perennial with 1 to several gray, cobwebby stems, up to 20" tall. The leaves are pinnately divided 2–3 times into 3–7 lobes, with the tips of the leaf blades curled. The inflorescence has 1 to many flower heads per stem, each approximately 1" long. The flowers heads have only disk flowers.

June–July

Habitat/Range: Open areas in mixed coniferous forest, subalpine forest, sagebrush scrub, pinyon-juniper woodland, and the alpine zone.

Comments: The species name honors the Scottish plant collector David Douglas (1799–1834), who was sent to North America in 1823 by the Horticultural Society of London to collect plants that could grow in English gardens.

KAREN WIESE

Elk Thistle

ELK THISTLE
Cirsium scariosum
Aster Family (Asteraceae)

Description: Hairy biennial up to 16" tall with very short, fleshy, and ridged stems, or lacking stems. The leaves are oblong, spiny, 4–16" long, and in a basal rosette. The inflorescence is a cluster of flower heads situated in the center of the basal rosette, close to the ground. The flower heads are 2" wide, with only disk flowers, and can be white or purple.

June–August

Habitat/Range: Wetlands in mixed coniferous forest, subalpine forest, pinyon-juniper woodland, and sagebrush scrub.

Comments: Some Native Americans ate the buds of thistles. Artichokes are also thistles, and this plant's buds are very similar to them.

CUT-LEAVED DAISY
Erigeron compositus
Aster Family (Asteraceae)

Description: Tufted, somewhat glandular perennial, up to 6" tall. The leaves are oblanceolate to spoon-shaped in outline, many-lobed, 2–3 lobed at the tips, crowded at the base, and up to 2" long. The inflorescence is a single flower head almost 1" wide, with white, pink, or blue ray flowers and yellow disk flowers. Sometimes only disk flowers are present.

July–August

Habitat/Range: Rocky places in subalpine forest and the alpine zone.

Comments: The species name is Latin for "compound," or "many parts," referring to the divided leaves. The name *daisy* refers only to those plants in the genus *Erigeron*.

KAREN WIESE

Cut-Leaved Daisy

COULTER'S DAISY
Erigeron coulteri
Aster Family (Asteraceae)

Description: Perennial 8–28" tall. The leaves are oblanceolate, 2–5" long, and often clasping the stem. The inflorescence is a cluster of 1–4 flower heads, 2" in diameter, with white ray flowers and yellow disk flowers.

July–August

Habitat/Range: Wetlands in mixed coniferous forest and subalpine forest.

Comments: The species name honors the Irish physician and naturalist Thomas Coulter (1793–1843), who was one of the important early botanical explorers in North America and the first botanist to collect in Arizona.

KAREN WIESE

Coulter's Daisy

KAREN WIESE

Popcorn Flower

POPCORN FLOWER
Cryptantha spp.
Borage Family (Boraginaceae)

Description: Hairy annual, biennial, or perennial, ascending to erect. The leaves are linear or oblong, opposite at the base and alternate along the stem. The inflorescence is a dense to open cyme that is coiled. Each flower is small and trumpet-shaped with 5 lobes, with a yellow, raised ring inside the throat.

March–August

Habitat/Range: Open areas in all plant communities.

Comments: The genus name is Greek for "hidden flowers," referring to the cleistogamous flowers of some species. In the field, it is difficult to distinguish between this genus and the related genus *Plagiobothrys.* The distinguishing characteristic between these two genera is a tiny scar on the nutlet. Telling them apart requires magnified views of the nutlets and the hairs.

KAREN CALLAHAN

Watercress

WATERCRESS
Rorippa nasturtium-aquaticum
Mustard Family (Brassicaceae)

Description: Aquatic perennial that is either submerged, floating, or prostrate on mud, up to 2' long. The plant has many leaves; these are pinnate, with 3–7 oblong to ovate leaflets. The plant roots freely at the nodes. The 4-petaled flowers, which occur at the top of the plant, are ⅜" across. The fruit is up to ½" long.

May–October

Habitat/Range: Wetlands in foothill woodland, pinyon-juniper woodland, mixed coniferous forest, and sagebrush scrub.

Comments: The plants are cultivated as edible greens.

NUTTALL'S SANDWORT
Minuartia nuttallii
Pink Family (Caryophyllaceae)

Description: Glandular, hairy, mat-forming perennial up to 8" tall. The small, needlelike leaves are dense along the stem. The 5-petaled, bell-shaped flowers occur in a cyme.

July–August

Habitat/Range: Open places, especially sandy and rocky areas, including serpentine-derived soils, in all plant communities.

Comments: The genus name honors the Spanish botanist and pharmacist J. Minuart (1693–1768). The species name honors the English printer and American naturalist Thomas Nuttall (1786–1859). The common name refers to the habitat of the plant.

RICHARD HANES

Nuttall's Sandwort

SARGENT'S CAMPION
Silene sargentii
Pink Family (Caryophyllaceae)

Description: Reclining to erect perennial, 4–8" tall, covered with glandular hairs. The leaves are linear, opposite, 1" long, and smaller toward the flower. The flowers are glandular, tubular, and have 5 petals, each with 2 lobes, and having inner petal-like appendages. The sepals are fused into a tube with prominent purple ribs. The petals can be white or pink.

July–August

Habitat/Range: Rocky areas in subalpine forest and the alpine zone.

Comments: Another common name, catchfly, is derived from the sticky hairs that discourage crawling insects, which are inefficient pollinators, from visiting the plant.

Sargent's Campion

Sierra Morning-Glory

SIERRA MORNING-GLORY
Calystegia malacophylla
Morning-Glory Family (Convolvulaceae)

Description: Densely hairy, reclining to ascending perennial, 4–40" long. The leaves are alternate, triangular, and 1–2" long. The flower has 2 bracts that almost conceal the calyx. The flower is pleated in bud and opens to a broad funnel, 1–2" long.

May–August

Habitat/Range: Open areas in foothill woodland and mixed coniferous forest.

Comments: The genus name is Greek for "concealing calyx," referring to bracts in this species. The species name is Latin for "soft leaf."

KAREN WIESE

Mountain Dogwood

MOUNTAIN DOGWOOD
Cornus nuttallii
Dogwood Family (Cornaceae)

Description: Deciduous tree up to 70' tall. The leaves are opposite, obovate, 2 ½–5" long, and turn crimson in autumn. The inflorescence consists of 4–7 showy, white, petal-like bracts, 2–3" across, with a cluster of small flowers in the middle. The fruits, which appear in the fall, are red ½" long, and occur in clusters.

April–July

Habitat/Range: Shaded, especially moist areas, in foothill woodland and mixed coniferous forest.

Comments: The genus name is Latin for "horn," referring to the wood, which is as hard as a horn. The species name honors the English printer and American naturalist Thomas Nuttall (1786–1859).

WHITE HEATHER
Cassiope mertensiana
Heath Family (Ericaceae)

Description: Low-growing, densely branched shrub up to 1' tall. The small, pointed leaves are slightly leathery and are imbricated (overlapped) on the stem. There are 5 red sepals above the nodding, bell-shaped flowers. The flowers are less than ¼" long and have 5 slightly reflexed lobes.

July–August

Habitat/Range: Wetlands and rocky places in subalpine forest and the alpine zone.

Comments: The genus name honors the Greek mythological queen of Ethiopia and mother of Andromeda. The species name honors the German botanist Franz Mertens (1764–1831). This plant was a favorite of naturalist John Muir, who wrote: "Here too . . . I met Cassiope growing in fringes among the battered rocks. No evangel among all the mountain plants speaks Nature's love more plainly than Cassiope."

KAREN WIESE

White Heather

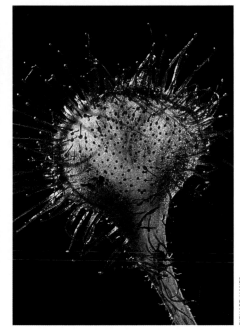

WIN & BOB EHRHART

RICHARD HANES

Round-Leaved Sundew

ROUND-LEAVED SUNDEW
Drosera rotundifolia
Sundew Family (Droseraceae)

Description: A small, uncommon insectivorous plant with a flower stalk 2–10" tall. The spoon-shaped leaves are arranged in a basal rosette, with each leaf up to ½" wide. On the upper surface of the leaves are gland-tipped hairs that secrete a sticky fluid. When an insect lands on the leaf, it gets stuck and the leaf folds around its prey and secretes digestive enzymes. This is an adaptation for life in a habitat that lacks nutrients. The 5-petaled flowers are less than ¼" long and arranged at the top of the flower stalk.

July–August

Habitat/Range: Wetlands (sphagnum bogs) in mixed coniferous forest.

Comments: The genus name is Greek for "dewy," referring to the dewlike glands tipping the hairs of the leaves. The species name means "round-leaved."

KAREN WIESE

Western Labrador Tea

WESTERN LABRADOR TEA
Ledum glandulosum
Heath Family (Ericaceae)

Description: Evergreen shrub, 3–5' tall. The leaves are leathery, oblong, up to 1 ½" long, and alternate on a soft-hairy stem. The leaves are glandular, and yellow-green beneath. At the end of the branch is a 3–4" wide, round-topped cluster of many ½" wide flowers with 5 petals and 8–10 exserted stamens.

June–August

Habitat/Range: Rocky places and wetlands in mixed coniferous forest, subalpine forest, and the alpine zone.

Comments: Contrary to the common name, this plant is poisonous to humans and live-stock. The species name is Latin for "glandular," referring to the leaves.

ONE-SIDED WINTERGREEN
Orthilia secunda
Heath Family (Ericaceae)

Description: Evergreen perennial up to 8" tall. The leaves are ovate and generally occur at the base; their margins range from entire to finely serrate. The inflorescence is an arched raceme of 1-sided flowers. The spherical flowers have 5 petals and an exserted style. The flowers can be white or pale green.

July–September

Habitat/Range: Shaded areas in mixed coniferous forest and subalpine forest.

Comments: The genus name is Greek for "straight spiral," referring to the 1-sided floral arrangement. The species name means "side-flowering."

KAREN WIESE

One-Sided Wintergreen

PINEDROPS
Pterospora andromedea
Heath Family (Ericaceae)

Description: Perennial with a sticky, slender, reddish brown flower stalk up to 4' tall, occurring either singly or in clusters. The nodding, bell-shaped flowers are ⅜" long. The flowers can appear red or brown as they age. The dry flower stalks may persist throughout the fall and winter into the following year. The small seeds of this plant are wind dispersed.

June–August

Habitat/Range: Shaded areas in mixed coniferous forest.

Comments: The genus name is Greek for "winged seed," referring to the wings on the microscopic seeds that assist seed dispersal. The species name honors Andromeda, the daughter of Cassiope in Greek mythology, who was tied to a rock to be devoured by a sea monster but was rescued by Perseus, son of Zeus.

Pinedrops

White-Veined Wintergreen

WHITE-VEINED WINTERGREEN
Pyrola picta
Heath Family (Ericaceae)

Description: Small, evergreen plant, 4–12" tall. The leaves are ovate, dark green, and up to 4" long, with white veins or mottling. The nodding, saucer-shaped flowers occur on a leafless flower stalk. Each flower is ½" long and has 5 petals and a downwardly curved, exserted style.

June–August

Habitat/Range: Shaded and dry areas in mixed coniferous forest, especially among ponderosa pines, and subalpine forest.

Comments: The genus name is Latin for "small pear," referring to the shape of the leaf. The common name refers to the evergreen leaves, which are green even in winter. Some Native Americans used the leaves as a poultice, applied to sores and bruises.

KAREN WIESE

Western Azalea

WESTERN AZALEA
Rhododendron occidentale
Heath Family (Ericaceae)

Description: Deciduous shrub, densely branched, 3–10' tall. The leaves are elliptic and up to 3 ½" long. The loosely funnel-shaped flowers are up to 2" across. The 5 petals are arranged irregularly with a yellow or salmon-colored blotch on the uppermost petal. The 5 stamens extend beyond the length of the flower. The flowers can be white or pink.

April–August

Habitat/Range: Wetlands, especially stream banks, in mixed coniferous forest.

Comments: The genus name is Greek for "rose tree." This is one of the two rhododendrons native to California; the other species is evergreen. Both the fragrance and the deep orange nectar guide lure one of its pollinators, the hawkmoth, to this plant.

LONG-STALKED CLOVER
Trifolium longipes
Pea Family (Fabaceae)

Description: Perennial, sprawling to erect, up to 16" long. The leaves are palmately compound, with 3 linear leaflets, 1" long. The inflorescence is a 1" wide sphere of densely clustered pea-family flowers. The flowers are ½–¾" long and can be white, purple, or white with purple tips.

June–September

Habitat/Range: Wetlands in mixed coniferous forest and sometimes in serpentine areas.

Comments: The genus name is Latin for "three leaves." The species name is Latin for "long-stalked." Some Native Americans ate the leaves after boiling them. Clover leaves and seeds are a good source of food for birds, squirrels, and deer. The larvae of the Mexican cloudywing butterfly (*Thorybes mexicana*) and the orange sulfur butterfly (*Colias eurytheme*) feed on the plant.

KAREN WIESE

Long-Stalked Clover

Alpine Gentian

ALPINE GENTIAN
Gentiana newberryi
Gentian Family (Gentianaceae)

Description: Perennial with 1 to several spreading stems, 2–4" tall. The leaves are spoon shaped and 1–2" long. There are 1–5 flowers per plant. The funnel-shaped corolla is 1–2" long; between each of the 4 fused petals is a fringed margin. There is a dark purple stripe on the exterior of each petal. The throat of the flower is sometimes dotted with green.

July–September

Habitat/Range: Wetlands, especially meadows, in subalpine forest and the alpine zone.

Comments: The species name honors the king of ancient Illyria, Gentius, whose army was defeated by the Romans in 168 B.C., and who is said to have discovered the power the plant had in healing his malaria-stricken troops. The species name honors John Strong Newberry, a botanist, paleontologist, and geologist who collected in California for the Williamson Railroad Survey from 1854 to 1856.

Monument Plant

MONUMENT PLANT
Swertia radiata
Gentian Family (Gentianaceae)

Description: Large perennial, 2–6' tall. The leaves are oblanceolate, 4–20" long, and are arranged along the stem in whorls of 3–7 leaves. The inflorescence is a 1–2' long panicle of many 4-petaled flowers, 1–2" wide. The open, saucer-shaped flowers have purple dots and twin hairy gland spots on each petal. The gland spots are nectar glands, which attract insects with a sweet odor, thereby increasing the chances for pollination.

July–August

Habitat/Range: Open areas in mixed coniferous forest and subalpine forest.

Comments: The genus name honors the Dutch herbalist E. Sweert, born in 1552. Though the fleshy root is bitter, Native Americans ate it raw, roasted, or boiled, often mixed with greens. Some floristic manuals list this plant as *Frasera speciosa*.

DRAPERIA
Draperia systyla
Waterleaf Family (Hydrophyllaceae)

Description: Soft-hairy, spreading to erect perennial, up to 16" long. The leaves are ovate, opposite, and up to 3" long. The inflorescence is a cluster of 10–20 funnel-shaped flowers, each ⅜–½" long. The flowers can appear pale violet.

May–August

Habitat/Range: Shaded, especially dry areas and rocky places in mixed coniferous forest and subalpine forest.

Comments: The genus name honors the nineteenth-century American historian and scientist John W. Draper. This genus, which only occurs in California, is monotypic—it contains only one species.

Draperia

Fivespot

FIVESPOT
Nemophila maculata
Waterleaf Family (Hydrophyllaceae)

Description: Annual, often sprawling plant up to 1' long. The leaves are 1" long, lobed, and arranged opposite each other on the stem. The saucer-shaped corolla is up to 2" wide and has a large purple spot on each of the 5 petal tips.

April–July

Habitat/Range: Open areas, especially meadows, in foothill woodland and mixed coniferous forest.

Comments: The genus name is Greek for "grove-loving," referring to its woodland habitat. The species name means "spot" in Latin and, like the common name, refers to the design on the petals.

KAREN WIESE

Timberline Phacelia; Silverleaf Phacelia

TIMBERLINE PHACELIA; SILVERLEAF PHACELIA
Phacelia hastata
Waterleaf Family (Hydrophyllaceae)

Description: Stiff-hairy, gray-green perennial, sprawling to erect, up to 20" long. The leaves are lanceolate to elliptic and occur at the base of the plant. The many bell-shaped flowers occur in a coiled cyme, and each flower is ⅜" long. The flowers can be white or lavender. The stamens extend beyond the corolla.

July–September

Habitat/Range: Rocky places in mixed coniferous forest, subalpine forest, sagebrush scrub, and the alpine zone.

Comments: The genus name is Greek for a "cluster," referring to the dense clusters of flowers that make the plant appear as if it is covered with caterpillars. The hairs on several species of *Phacelia* can cause an irritation in susceptible individuals.

CALIFORNIA SKULLCAP
Scutellaria californica
Mint Family (Lamiaceae)

Description: Hairy perennial with a square stem, 6–30" tall. The leaves are 1" long and ovate with entire margins. The flowers occur in pairs in the axils of the upper leaves. The 2-lipped calyx has a ridge on the upper side. The corolla is 2-lipped, with the upper and lower lips the same length. The upper lip is hoodlike over the reproductive parts. The 3-lobed lower lip has a middle petal that acts as a landing pad for pollinating insects.

May–July

Habitat/Range: Open areas in foothill woodland, and mixed coniferous forest.

Comments: The genus name is Latin for "tray," referring to the ridge on the upper side of the calyx. The common name refers to the calyx, which, when turned upside down, resembles a helmet. Herbalists have used scullcap as a sedative and a treatment for rabies.

KAREN CALLAHAN

California Skullcap

WHITE HEDGE-NETTLE
Stachys albens
Mint Family (Lamiaceae)

Description: Densely white-woolly perennial that is 1–6' tall. The leaves are opposite, triangular, 1–4" long, and extend at right angles from the 4-sided stem. The inflorescence is a spike of dense clusters of 6–12 flowers with cobweblike hairs. The flower is tubular, 2-lipped, and ½" long, with the upper lip shorter than the lower lip. The petals may have purple veins or white dots; these are nectar guides that guide insects into the corolla for pollination.

June–October

Habitat/Range: Wetlands in mixed coniferous forest and subalpine forest.

Comments: The genus name is Greek for "ear of grain," referring to the inflorescence, which is arranged like an ear of corn. The species name is Latin for "white," referring to the dense white hairs.

White Hedge-Nettle

FAIRY LANTERN; WHITE GLOBE LILY
Calochortus albus
Lily Family (Liliaceae)

Description: Perennial, rising 8–28" tall from a bulb. A single linear leaf grows from the base of the plant, and there are several stem leaves. The inflorescence is a cluster of nodding, spherical flowers, each flower up to 1" long. Inside the flower, at the base of the 3 petals, are tiny nectar glands that attract pollinating insects. Above the nectar glands are silky hairs that gently brush pollen off of a visiting insect, pollinating the plant. The fruit is broad, 3-winged, and 1–2" long.

April–June

Habitat/Range: Open and shaded areas in foothill woodland and mixed coniferous forest.

Comments: The genus name is Greek for "beautiful grass"; the species name is Latin for "white," referring to the flower color.

Fairy Lantern; White Globe Lily

Leichtlin's Mariposa Lily

LAURIE FRIEDMAN

LEICHTLIN'S MARIPOSA LILY
Calochortus leichtlinii
Lily Family (Liliaceae)

Description: Perennial rising up to 2' from a bulb. The leaves are linear, basal, 4–6" long, and often withered. The inflorescence is an erect single flower or cluster of 2–5 flowers. Each bell-shaped flower is ½–1 ½" long and has 3 sepals and 3 petals. Inside the flower, each petal has a deep red spot above the nectar gland, and near the nectar gland are short hairs that brush pollen off of visiting insects. The fruit is erect, narrow, ¼" long, and 3-winged.

June–August

Habitat/Range: Open areas in mixed coniferous forest and subalpine forest.

Comments: The genus name honors the German horticulturist Max Leichtlin (1831–1910), who introduced American plants to the gardeners of Europe during the latter half of the 1800s. The common name is Spanish for "butterfly," referring to the colorful pattern of the petals. The roasted bulbs were an important food for Native Americans of the Sierra Nevada. The seeds and young leaves were eaten as well.

Soap Plant; Amole

SOAP PLANT; AMOLE
Chlorogalum pomeridianum
Lily Family (Liliaceae)

Description: Perennial, rising 2–5' from a large bulb. The bulb is 6" long with a very fibrous outer coat. The leaves are linear, basal, and up to 30" long, with wavy margins. The inflorescence is a branched panicle of 15–25 flowers. The flowers are ½–1" wide, white, with a green or purple midvein. Each flower has 3 petal-like sepals and 3 petals. The flowers, which are pollinated by moths, open in the evening and close by midmorning.

April–May

Habitat/Range: Open areas in foothill woodland.

Comments: The genus name is Greek for "green milk" or "green juice," referring to liquid in the root. Some Native Americans had many uses for the bulbs. The fibers that cover the bulb were made into brushes. The uncooked bulbs contain saponins (lather-producing components), so they were grated and used to wash clothes. Crushed bulbs were put in streams to produce a lather that would stun fish, making it easy to gather the fish for food. The bulbs were eaten, but only after boiling them to remove the saponins. The larvae of the brown elfin butterfly (*Callophrys augustinus iroides*) feed on this plant.

KAREN WIESE

Bride's Bonnet; Queen Cup

BRIDE'S BONNET; QUEEN CUP
Clintonia uniflora
Lily Family (Liliaceae)

Description: Perennial up to 6" tall with 2–3 oblanceolate or elliptic leaves. The inflorescence consists of 1–2 flowers, 1 ¼" wide, on a flower stalk that rarely exceeds the height of the leaves. Each flower has 3 petal-like sepals and 3 petals.

May–July

Habitat/Range: Shaded areas in mixed coniferous forest.

Comments: The genus name honors the naturalist and governor of New York De Witt Clinton (1769–1828). The species name means "one-flowered."

PLAINLEAF FAWN LILY
Erythronium purpurascens
Lily Family (Liliaceae)

Description: Perennial up to 8" tall, from a bulb. The leaves are basal, lanceolate, 2–6" long, with wavy margins. The inflorescence is a raceme of 1–6 flowers. Each nodding flower is 1" across and has 3 petal-like sepals and 3 petals that are all lanceolate. Each perianth part has a yellow base, is recurved, and turns purple with age.

May–July

Habitat/Range: Open areas and rocky places in mixed coniferous forest.

Comments: The genus name is Greek for "red," referring to the flower color of some species. The species name is Latin for "purple," referring to the final color of the flowers.

RICHARD HANES

Plainleaf Fawn Lily

WASHINGTON LILY
Lilium washingtonianum
Lily Family (Liliaceae)

Description: Perennial rising up to 6' from a bulb. The leaves are oblanceolate, 1–5" long, and grow in whorls along the stem. There are as many as 26 nodding, trumpet-shaped flowers, 3–5" wide, with a delightful fragrance. Each flower has 3 petal-like sepals and 3 petals, with pink spots in the throat or center of the flower. The flowers will often turn pink as they age.

July–August

Habitat/Range: Open areas in mixed coniferous forest.

Comments: The species name honors the former first lady Martha Washington (1732–1802). This species has the largest flowers of all the native lilies in California.

Washington Lily

STEVE MATSON

FALSE SOLOMON'S SEAL
Smilacina racemosa
Lily Family (Liliaceae)

Description: Perennial 1–3' tall. The leaves are alternate, ovate, and 3–8" long. The inflorescence is a panicle of more than 20 tiny, star-shaped flowers. Each flower is less that ¼" wide and has 3 petal-like sepals and 3 petals. The fruit is a cluster of purple-dotted, red berries that are ¼" in diameter, have 1–3 seeds inside, and are poisonous.

April–June

Habitat/Range: Wetlands, especially stream banks, in coniferous forest.

Comments: The common name of this plant refers to a similar-looking plant in the eastern United States called Solomon's seal. The name refers to an Old World species whose leaf scars resemble the seal of the biblical King Solomon.

KAREN WIESE

False Solomon's Seal

KAREN WIESE

Corn Lily

CORN LILY
Veratrum californicum var. *californicum*
Lily Family (Liliaceae)

Description: Perennial 3–6' tall, often growing in masses. The leaves are 6–12" long, ovate, and alternate on the stem. The inflorescence is a panicle of many saucer-shaped flowers. Each flower is ¾" wide with 3 petal-like sepals and 3 petals. At the base of each perianth part is a Y-shaped green nectar gland.

July–August

Habitat/Range: Wetlands, especially meadows, in mixed coniferous forest and subalpine forest.

Comments: The genus name is Latin for "dark root." All parts of this plant are toxic to humans and livestock, causing a reduced heart rate and potentially death. Pregnant sheep grazing on this plant can give birth to lambs with birth defects. The Washoe Native Americans used the cured roots of this plant to make a tea that was used as birth control. The dried and powdered roots were used as an insecticide.

BEAR-GRASS; INDIAN BASKET-GRASS
Xerophyllum tenax
Lily Family (Liliaceae)

Description: Perennial up to 5' tall. This plant has many tough, grasslike leaves occurring at the base of the plant in a dense clump. The inflorescence is a dense raceme of many small flowers. Each flower is ⅜" wide and has 3 petal-like sepals and 3 petals.

May–August

Habitat/Range: Open areas in mixed coniferous forest.

Comments: The genus name is Greek for "dry leaf," referring to the tough, persistent leaves. Some Native Americans used the leaves, as is, or dyed with the bark of the alder, to weave overlay patterns on baskets.

DANN MCCRIGHT

Bear-Grass; Indian Basket-Grass

Our Lord's Candle; Yucca

OUR LORD'S CANDLE; YUCCA
Yucca whipplei
Lily Family (Liliaceae)

Description: Treelike shrub, up to 12' tall. The leaves are linear, stiff, up to 3' long, forming a basal rosette. The inflorescence is a dense panicle of nodding flowers on a tall flower stalk. Each spherical flower has 3 petal-like sepals and 3 petals. The perianth parts are white, often with purple tips.

May–June

Habitat/Range: Open areas in lower elevations in the southern Sierra Nevada, especially on the eastern slope.

Comments: Some Native Americans used yucca roots for food, soap, and to make medicine that was used internally and externally to treat a variety of ailments. The leaves were used in basketry and to make cordage. The flowers are pollinated at night by small moths that lay their eggs in the ovary of the flower. The growing larvae eat some of the developing seeds, but this cost to the plant is outweighed by the benefit of the moths' pollination.

KAREN CALLAHAN

White Meadowfoam

WHITE MEADOWFOAM
Limnanthes alba
Meadowfoam Family (Limnanthaceae)

Description: Annual, up to 1' tall. The leaves are linear to ovate, compound, and less than 4" long; there are 5–9 leaflets, which are linear to ovate in outline and entire to deeply 3-lobed. The flowers are saucer shaped, up to 1" wide. Each of the 4–5 petals are slightly notched at the tip.

April–June

Habitat/Range: Wetlands, especially vernal pools, in foothill woodland.

Comments: The genus name is Greek for "marsh flower," referring to the plant's habitat. The species name is Latin for "white," referring to the flower color.

PHANTOM ORCHID
Cephalanthera austiniae
Orchid Family (Orchidaceae)

Description: Non-photosynthesizing, fragrant perennial, 8–21" tall, that is white when it is young and yellow or brown as it ages. The leaves are 1–2" long, small, and scalelike. The inflorescence is a 2–6" long raceme of flowers, each 1 ¼" wide. The flowers have 3 elliptic sepals and 3 petals. The 2 upper petals are curved inward and the lower petal is lip shaped with a yellow surface that attracts pollinating insects.

May–June

Habitat/Range: Shaded areas in decomposed litter of rich soil in mixed coniferous forest.

Comments: The genus name is Greek for "headlike anther," referring to the position of the anther. This orchid is mycotrophic—it obtains food from a mycorrhizal relationship with fungi. The orchid obtains its nutrients through a network of fungal filaments that invades its roots and extends throughout the soil.

KAREN WIESE

Phantom Orchid

California Lady's Slipper

CALIFORNIA LADY'S SLIPPER
Cypripedium californicum
Orchid Family (Orchidaceae)

Description: Uncommon perennial, 6–24" tall, often growing in colonies. The leaves are alternate, lanceolate, and 3–5" long. The inflorescence has up to 14 flowers, each with a distinguishing pouchlike lower petal that is white. The 2 remaining lateral petals are yellowish white. There are 3 greenish yellow sepals: 2 fused sepals under the lip, and 1 upright and ovate.

May–June

Habitat/Range: Wetlands in mixed coniferous forest.

Comments: The genus name is from the Greek words for Aphrodite (the Greek goddess of love), and "foot"—thus "Aphrodite's foot" or "lady's slipper," referring to the shape of the flower. This orchid grows almost exclusively on serpentine rocks or in a serpentine-based substrate.

KAREN WIESE

Mountain Lady's Slipper

MOUNTAIN LADY'S SLIPPER
Cypripedium montanum
Orchid Family (Orchidaceae)

Description: Uncommon perennial, up to 2' tall. The leaves are 2–6" long, alternate, and elliptic. The inflorescence has 1–3 flowers that are up to 4" wide, each with a distinguishing pouchlike lower petal that is white with purple veins (nectar guides) inside. Inside the rear of the pouch are fine hairs that help pollinators exit. The 2 lateral petals are lanceolate, purple, 1–2" long, and twisted. There are 3 purple sepals; the 2 lower ones are fused, and the upper sepal is 1–2" long, wavy-edged, and usually purple.

May–August

Habitat/Range: Shady areas, both moist and dry, in mixed coniferous forest.

Comments: The genus name means "Aphrodite's foot" or "lady's slipper," referring to the shape of the flower. The species name is Latin for "pertaining to the mountains," referring to its habitat. This is the largest orchid flower in California. The orchid family has over 18,000 species worldwide. Real vanilla comes from the fruit of a tropical orchid (*Vanilla planifolia*); vanillin is a synthetic substitute.

_AURIE FRIEDMAN

White-Flowered Bog-Orchid; Sierra Rein-Orchid

WHITE-FLOWERED BOG-ORCHID; SIERRA REIN-ORCHID

Plantanthera leucostachys
Orchid Family (Orchidaceae)

Description: Perennial, 6–36" tall, often growing in large colonies. The leaves are lanceolate and 4–8" long. The inflorescence is a dense cluster of flowers that occur along most of the flower stalk. The flowers have 3 sepals and 3 petals. The upper sepal and 2 upper petals form a hood. The 2 lower sepals are lateral. The lower petal forms a tapered lip that hangs down and has a spur that curves outward under the lip.

June–September

Habitat/Range: Wetlands in mixed coniferous forest and subalpine forest.

Comments: The genus name is Greek for "wide anther," referring to the fused stamens and style that form a wide column. The species name is Latin for "white spike," referring to the inflorescence. One of the common names is derived from the petal spur that resembles the reins of a horse's bridle. Ron Coleman, in his book *The Wild Orchids of California*, reports that this species can have more than 100 flowers per plant, and that one herbarium specimen bore 248 flowers.

KAREN WIESE

Prickly Poppy; Chicalote

PRICKLY POPPY; CHICALOTE
Argemone munita
Poppy Family (Papaveraceae)

Description: Annual or perennial, spiny, with yellow sap, 2–5' tall. The leaves are alternate, oblanceolate, deeply serrate, and 3–6" long. The saucer-shaped flowers bloom at the top of the plant. The flowers have 3–6 petals and are 2–5" wide. In the center of the flower are over 150 orange stamens. The oval fruit is up to 1" long with numerous spines.

June–September

Habitat/Range: Open areas in mixed coniferous forest, pinyon-juniper woodland, and sagebrush scrub in the eastern Sierra Nevada.

Comments: The genus name is Greek for "cataract of the eye," referring a condition supposedly cured by the juice of another poppylike plant of the same name.

SIERRA CORYDALIS; FITWEED
Corydalis caseana ssp. *caseana*
Poppy Family (Papaveraceae)

Description: Uncommon perennial up to 3' tall, covered with a waxy coating. The leaves are dissected and up to 1' long. The inflorescence is a dense, narrow raceme or panicle of flowers. Each flower has 4 petals. The outer 2 petals are keeled, with the upper petal spurred at the base. The 2 inner petals are attached at the tip.

June–August

Habitat/Range: Shaded, especially moist areas in mixed coniferous forest and subalpine forest.

Comments: The genus name is Greek for "crested lark." This plant is on the California Native Plant Society's "Watch" list for sensitive species. Sierra corydalis is poisonous to humans and livestock.

KAREN CALLAHAN

Sierra Corydalis; Fitweed

EDWARD RINGROSE

Granite-Gilia; Prickly Phlox

GRANITE-GILIA; PRICKLY PHLOX

Leptodactylon pungens
Phlox Family (Polemoniaceae)

Description: Sprawling, aromatic, and generally hairy subshrub, 4–12" tall. The leaves are alternate, with 3–7 linear, spiny-tipped lobes—hence one of its common names, prickly phlox. The flowers are ½" wide, funnel shaped with 4–6 lobes, and usually open in the evening.

May–August

Habitat/Range: Open areas and rocky places in mixed coniferous forest, subalpine forest, and the alpine zone.

Comments: The genus name is Greek for "narrow finger," and the species name is Latin for "sharp-pointed"; both names describe the leaves.

Nude Buckwheat

NUDE BUCKWHEAT
Eriogonum nudum
Buckwheat Family (Polygonaceae)

Description: Perennial, up to 42" tall. The spoon-shaped leaves are basal, leaving a naked stem, hence the common name. The leaves are 3" long; the upper surface is green, and the lower surface has white feltlike hairs. The inflorescence is a small, round cluster, 1" wide, of many small flowers. Instead of petals, each flower has petal-like sepals, which can be white or yellow.

June–September

Habitat/Range: Open areas in all plant communities in the Sierra Nevada.

Comments: The genus name is Greek for "wool knee," referring to the hairy nodes of many species. Buckwheats are excellent bee plants. The larvae of the acmon blue butterfly (*Plebejus acmon*), the square-spotted blue butterfly (*Euphilotes battoides*), and the blue copper butterfly (*Lycaena heteronea*) feed on this plant.

WESTERN BISTORT; LADIES' THUMB
Polygonum bistortoides
Buckwheat Family (Polygonaceae)

Description: Perennial that grows 8–28" tall from a bulblike rhizome. The leaves are oblong, 2–19" long, and occur along the lower half of the stem. The inflorescence is a dense, oblong cluster of flowers, ¾–2" long, that occurs on a leafless stem. Instead of petals, each flower has petal-like sepals that can be white or pink. The stamens extend beyond the flower.

June–August

Habitat/Range: Wetlands, especially meadows, in mixed coniferous forest and subalpine forest.

Comments: The genus name is Greek for "many knees," referring to the numerous swollen nodes on some species. The common name refers to a similar European genus named *Bistorta*. Some Native Americans ate the cooked leaves and roots, and they ground the seeds into a flour. The root was also crushed to make a poultice for sores and boils.

Western Bistort; Ladies' Thumb

Oval-Leaved Eriogonum

OVAL-LEAVED ERIOGONUM
Eriogonum ovalifolium
Buckwheat Family (Polygonaceae)

Description: White-woolly, perennial, mat-forming plant, 6–12" tall and 1–16" wide. The leaves are woolly, elliptic, up to 2" long, and basal. The inflorescence is a cluster of flowers that is ½–1" in diameter, positioned at the top of a leafless stem. Instead of petals, each flower has petal-like sepals. The flowers can be white, purple, or yellow, turning burgundy with age.

May–August

Habitat/Range: Open areas in mixed coniferous forest, subalpine forest, pinyon-juniper woodland, sagebrush scrub, and the alpine zone.

Comments: The genus name is Greek for "wool knee," referring to the hairy nodes of many species. The species name is Latin for "oval-leaved."

Kellogg's Lewisia

KELLOGG'S LEWISIA
Lewisia kelloggii
Purslane Family (Portulacaceae)

Description: Perennial, up to 3" tall. The many leaves are arranged in a rosette and are spoon-shaped or obovate and up to 3 ½" long. The inflorescence is a solitary flower often exserted from the leaves. Each flower is up to 1" long and has 2 sepal-like bracts, 2 sepals, and 5–9 petals. The flowers can be white or pink.

June–July

Habitat/Range: Open areas, especially on decomposed granite and slate, in mixed coniferous forest and subalpine forest.

Comments: The genus name honors Meriwether Lewis (1774–1809), leader of the 1804–1806 Lewis and Clark Expedition. The species name honors Albert Kellogg (1813–1887), California botanist and physician.

STEVE MATSON

Drummond's Anemone

DRUMMOND'S ANEMONE
Anemone drummondii
Buttercup Family (Ranunculaceae)

Description: Perennial, up to 10" tall. The leaves are dissected, up to 6" long, and basal. The inflorescence can have 1–3 flowers, each on a flower stalk. Instead of petals, the flower has 5–8 petal-like sepals that are ¾" long, and many styles. The flower can be white or blue. The fruit is a dense cluster of woolly styles that resembles a mop.

May–August

Habitat/Range: Rocky places in mixed coniferous forest and subalpine forest.

Comments: The genus name is the ancient Greek name for this plant, which is derived from the Greek word for "wind." The species name honors the Scottish botanist Thomas Drummond (1790–1835), who was sent to America by British horticultural institutions to collect plants. Some Native Americans crushed the leaves to make a poultice to treat rheumatism.

KAREN WIESE

Coville's Columbine

COVILLE'S COLUMBINE
Aquilegia pubescens
Buttercup Family (Ranunculaceae)

Description: Perennial, up to 20" tall. The leaves are deeply 3-lobed and occur mostly on the lower half of the stem. The flowers are nearly 2" long, erect, with 5 cream to pink, petal-like sepals, and 5 cream to pink petals that form spurs that are reflexed between the sepals. The numerous stamens extend beyond the flower, making pollination easy.

June–August

Habitat/Range: Open and rocky areas in sub-alpine forest and the alpine zone.

Comments: The origin of the genus name is uncertain; possibly, it is from the Latin for "eagle," referring to the spurs that suggest claws, or from *aquilegus*, "water-drawer," from the habitat the plant prefers. Coville's columbine and crimson columbine will hybridize to produce plants with characteristics of both.

MARSH MARIGOLD
Caltha leptosepala
Buttercup Family (Ranunculaceae)

Description: Perennial, 1–14" tall. The leaves are heart shaped, ¾–3 ½" wide, and on a 1–10" stalk. The solitary or occasionally 2-flowered inflorescence is on a flower stalk up to 1' tall. The saucer-shaped flowers are ¾–1 ½" wide, have no petals, but have 5–11 petal-like sepals that are arranged symmetrically around many yellow stamens and pistils.

May–July

Habitat/Range: Wetlands in mixed coniferous forest and subalpine forest.

Comments: The genus name is from the Latin name for another plant named "marigold." The species name is Latin for "slender sepals," referring to the many slender petal-like sepals. Although the leaves are edible when cooked, the uncooked leaves can cause the skin to blister and burn.

KAREN WIESE

Marsh Marigold

DEER BRUSH
Ceanothus intergerrimus
Buckthorn (Rhamnaceae)

Description: Shrub, up to 13' tall—erect or spreading. The leaves are lanceolate to ovate, and alternate each other on the stem. The upper side of the leaf is darker than the lower, which can be covered with fine, white hairs. Three main veins connect at the base of the leaf. The inflorescence is a branched cluster of white or blue, saucer-shaped flowers. The flowers have petal-like sepals and 5 spoon-shaped petals. The fruit is 3-chambered, round, with 3 seeds.

May–July

Habitat/Range: Open areas in mixed coniferous forest.

Comments: The genus name is Greek for "thorny plant," referring to the thorns on several species. Some Native Americans in the Sierra Nevada hardened the branches with fire, then used these as digging sticks to unearth edible underground plant parts.

Deer Brush

Mountain Misery

MOUNTAIN MISERY
Chamaebatia foliolosa
Rose Family (Rosaceae)

Description: Aromatic and glandular evergreen shrub that forms dense clusters, up to 3' tall. The leaves are pinnate and finely divided, 1–4" long, and obovate in outline. The saucer-shaped flowers have 5 petals and many stamens.

May–July

Habitat/Range: Shaded areas in mixed coniferous forest.

Comments: The scientific name is Greek for "low bramble," referring to its growth habit. The species name is Latin for "having leaflets," referring to the compound leaves. The common name comes from the plant's resin, which sticks unpleasantly to clothing. The Miwok Indians called the shrub *kit-kit-dizze* and used the leaves to make a tea to treat rheumatism, chicken pox, measles, and smallpox.

LAURIE FRIEDMAN

Dusky Horkelia

DUSKY HORKELIA
Horkelia fusca
Rose Family (Rosaceae)

Description: Slightly hairy-glandular perennial, 6–20" tall. The leaves are pinnate, with 6–30 lobed leaflets, and occur mostly along the bottom half of the stem. The inflorescence is a headlike cluster of 5–30 flowers; each flower is ⅝" wide and has 5 wedge-shaped petals alternating with 5 sepals.

May–August

Habitat/Range: Open areas, especially meadow edges, in mixed coniferous forest and subalpine forest.

Comments: The genus name honors the German plant physiologist Johann Horkel (1769–1846). The larvae of the Edith's copper butterfly (*Lycaena editha*) feed on the leaves.

ROCK STAR; WOODLAND STAR
Lithophragma glabrum
Saxifrage Family (Saxifragaceae)

Description: Perennial, up to 10" tall. The leaves are basal and deeply 3-lobed. The bell-shaped flowers are in loose clusters of 1–7 along the flower stem. The flowers are ¼" long, with 5 white or pink petals that have 4–5 deep lobes. Late in the season, red "bulblets" may form near the flower. These bulblets will fall to the ground and can sprout.

April–July

Habitat/Range: Open areas in mixed coniferous forest, subalpine forest, and sagebrush scrub.

Comments: The genus name is Greek for "rock fence," referring to the plant's habitat. The species name is Latin for "smooth," referring to the texture of the entire plant.

KAREN WIESE

Rock Star: Woodland Star

GRASS-OF-PARNASSUS
Parnassia californica
Saxifrage Family (Saxifragaceae)

Description: Perennial plant up to 18" tall. The leaves are spoon-shaped and up to 5" long. The saucer-shaped flowers are 1 ½" wide and are solitary on 6–24" stems. Each flower has 5 round petals with green veins. In the center of the flower are 5 stamens. There are also 5 fringed staminodes, stamens that do not produce pollen, which mimic nectar glands. Insects are attracted to the staminodes and wind up pollinating the plant.

July–October

Habitat/Range: Wetlands in foothill woodland, mixed coniferous forest, and subalpine forest.

Comments: The genus name and common name refer to Mount Parnassus in Greece, the mythological home to the nine muses of song and poetry.

Grass-of-Parnassus

TINCTURE PLANT
Collinsia tinctoria
Figwort Family (Scrophulariaceae)

Description: Glandular annual, up to 2' tall. The leaves are opposite, lanceolate, up to 3" long, and hairy beneath. The inflorescence consists of flowers in whorls. Each flower is tubular, 1" long, and 2-lipped; the upper lip is 2-lobed, white, lavender, or purple spotted, and the lower lip is 3-lobed and white to rose-purple.

May–August

Habitat/Range: Rocky areas in foothill woodland and coniferous forest.

Comments: The genus honors the Philadelphia botanist Zaccheus Collins (1764–1831). The crushed flowers, leaves, and stems of this plant stain yellow-brown.

Tincture Plant

RICHARD HANES

Slender Bird's-Beak

SLENDER BIRD'S-BEAK
Cordylanthus tenuis
Figwort Family (Scrophulariaceae)

Description: Annual, up to 42" tall, often sticky, and with many slender branches. The linear leaves are up to 2 ½" long. The flowers occur in clusters of 1–7. The corolla is shaped like a bird's beak, with the upper lip pointed and the lower lip in a pouch roughly the same size as the upper lip. The white to yellow flowers have a maroon blotch.

July–September

Habitat/Range: Open areas, often in serpentine soils, in foothill woodland and mixed coniferous forest.

Comments: The genus name is Greek for "club-shaped flower." The species name means "slender." Plants in the genus *Cordylanthus* are green root parasites. These plants photosynthesize but also supplement water and nutrient uptake from the root system of a nearby host plant.

GAPING PENSTEMON
Keckiella breviflora
Figwort Family (Scrophulariaceae)

Description: Many-branched shrub growing to 6' tall that appears to have a waxy coating on the leaves. The leaves are opposite, lanceolate, and up to 1 ½" long. The inflorescence is a panicle of tubular flowers. The flowers are ¾" long and 2-lipped. The upper lip is curved in the shape of a beak and the lower lip has 3 reflexed lobes.

May–July

Habitat/Range: Rocky places in foothill woodland and mixed coniferous forest.

Comments: The genus name honors the California botanist David Daniels Keck (1903–1995). The lobes have purple or pink lines that serve as nectar guides for pollinating insects. The insects follow the dark lines to the nectar. As they gather nectar, they simultaneously gather and disseminate pollen.

RICHARD HANES

Gaping Penstemon

Jimson Weed; Thorn-Apple

KAREN CALLAHAN

JIMSON WEED; THORN-APPLE
Datura wrightii
Nightshade Family (Solanaceae)

Description: Spreading annual or perennial, with a strong odor, up to 5' long. The leaves are ovate, up to 8" long, and often with wavy margins. The funnel-shaped flowers are solitary in the axils of the branches and are up to 8" long. The corolla has 5 evenly spaced points or lobes, ¾" long on the edge. The fruit is egg-shaped with prickles, 1" wide, and filled with tan seeds.

April–October

Habitat/Range: Open areas in foothill woodland.

Comments: The genus name is the ancient Hindu name for a related species. All species are highly toxic. The Yokut Indians in the Sierra Nevada, as well as other tribes throughout the southwestern United States, used this plant in special ceremonies. They used the roots to make a drink that was consumed as a once-in-a-lifetime ceremonial event, or when a medical situation warranted a strong painkiller.

KAREN WIESE

California Valerian

CALIFORNIA VALERIAN
Valeriana californica
Valerian Family (Valerianaceae)

Description: Perennial, 10–20" tall. The leaves are generally deeply 3-lobed and 5" long. The inflorescence is an umbel-like cluster of flowers, each less than ¼" long. The funnel-shaped flowers have 5 lobes and a spur near the base. Three stamens are exserted from the flower.

July–September

Habitat/Range: Shaded areas, especially meadows, in mixed coniferous forest and subalpine forest.

Comments: The genus name is Latin for "strength," referring to the medicinal properties, or else referring to Valerian, a Roman emperor. The Pied Piper of Hamelin is reported to have used a European valerian to draw rats out of his town. Some Native Americans used the boiled roots as food and the plant to treat stomach problems.

MACLOSKEY'S VIOLET
Viola macloskeyi
Violet Family (Violaceae)

Description: Perennial, 6" tall, often forming dense patches. The leaves are ovate, up to 2" long, and on a leaf stalk that can be up to 4" long originating at the base of the plant. The nodding, funnel-shaped, 5-petaled flowers are ½–¾" wide on a flower stalk 6" tall. The 3 bottom petals are joined into a spur and have purple nectar guides that attract flying insects to the nectar glands inside the spur. Insects pollinate the plant while trying to obtain nectar.

May–August

Habitat/Range: Wetlands in mixed coniferous forest and subalpine forest.

Comments: The genus name is the ancient Latin name of this plant. This is one of the few native violets with a fragrance.

KAREN WIESE

Macloskey's Violet

Brown and Green Flowers

This section includes flowers that range from pale green to purplish brown. This section also includes flowers that lack colorful petals. Some of the flowers included in this section are mottled. If you cannot find the flower you are looking for here, you may want to check the white or purple sections.

KAREN CALLAHAN

Hartweg's Wild-Ginger

HARTWEG'S WILD-GINGER
Asarum hartwegii
Pipevine Family (Aristolochiaceae)

Description: Perennial that spreads from a horizontal rhizome near the soil surface and forms a loose mat. The leaves are heart shaped and often have white mottling. The unusual flowers are difficult to see at first glance; they are located just above ground level. The 3 lobes of the calyx are long, pointed, and reflexed and up to 2 ½" long. The outer surface of the calyx is hairy. There are no petals.

May–June

Habitat/Range: Open areas in mixed coniferous forest.

Comments: Though the plant is not related to the commercial ginger (*Zingiber officinale*), wild-ginger is aromatic, reminiscent of ginger, and the root can be used as a spice.

BIG SAGEBRUSH
Artemisia tridentata
Aster Family (Asteraceae)

Description: Aromatic, gray-woolly shrub, up to 9' tall. The leaves are wedge-shaped, 1" long, and 3-toothed. The inflorescence is a cluster of densely hairy, small disk flowers.

Habitat/Range: Open areas in pinyon-juniper woodland and sagebrush scrub.

Comments: The genus name honors Artemis, Greek goddess of untamed nature. The species name is Latin for "three-toothed," referring to the leaves. Some Native Americans made a tea from the leaves of sagebrush as a remedy for common colds and used the leaves as an inhalant in sweat lodges.

Big Sagebrush

FENDLER'S MEADOW-RUE
Thalictrum fendleri
Buttercup Family (Ranunculaceae)

Description: A perennial 2–6' tall, with separate female and male plants. The margins of the lobed leaves are gently serrate. Most of the leaves are on the lower half of the stem. There are no petals on either female or male flowers, but each has 4–5 petal-like sepals. The female (pistillate) flowers have about 10 densely clustered pistils; the male (staminate) flowers have dangling clusters of stamens. Both types of flowers are ½" long.

May–August

Habitat/Range: Open or shaded areas, especially meadows, in mixed coniferous forest.

Comments: The genus name was given by the Greek physician and botanist Dioscorides. Some Native Americans made a tea from the roots to treat colds and made a shampoo from the powdered dried roots.

Fendler's Meadow-Rue

EDWARD RINGROSE

Arctic Willow

ARCTIC WILLOW
Salix arctica
Willow Family (Salicaceae)

Description: Mat-forming, sprawling, dwarf alpine shrub only 4" tall. The leaves are elliptic and are soft-hairy when young. The inflorescence is a dense, upright catkin, up to 2" tall, of either female or male flowers, occurring along the stem.

July–August

Habitat/Range: Wetlands, especially moist banks and meadows, in the upper elevations of the subalpine forest and the alpine zone.

Comments: Members of the genus *Salix* were an important basketry material for Native Americans. The inner bark contains salicylates, compounds similar to those found in aspirin, and was used in a tea or as a poultice by some Native Americans for a painkiller.

BISHOP'S CAP; MITERWORT
Mitella breweri
Saxifrage Family (Saxifragaceae)

Description: Slender perennial, 4–12" tall. The leaves are basal, round, and 1–3" wide with shallow lobes. The inflorescence, a loose cluster of flowers along a flower stalk, blooms from bottom to top. Each flower has 5–9 unusual threadlike branched petals alternating with the stamens. The saucer-shaped flowers are ½" wide.

June–August

Habitat/Range: Shaded areas and wetlands in mixed coniferous forest and subalpine forest.

Comments: The genus name is Latin for "small cap," referring to the shape of the young fruit. The species name honors William H. Brewer, the first person to botanize extensively in the Sierra Nevada in the 1860s. Brewer worked as a botanist with the California State Geological Survey. Both common names refer to the triangular fruit that encloses the seeds. The fruit resembles a miter, the tall pointed hat worn by Catholic bishops. The word *wort* is Middle English for "plant."

KAREN WIESE

Bishop's Cap; Miterwort

BROWN BELLS
Fritillaria micrantha
Lily Family (Liliaceae)

Description: Perennial rising up to 3' from a bulb. The linear to lanceolate leaves occur in 1–3 whorls of 4–6 below and are alternate above. The 4–10 nodding, bell-shaped flowers are 1" wide and have 3 petal-like sepals and 3 petals; each of these is purple or greenish white and sometimes faintly mottled, with white tufts on the perianth tips. The style is in three parts.

April–June

Habitat/Range: Dry areas in mixed coniferous forest.

Comments: The species name is Latin for "dice box," referring to the shape of the fruit. The species name is Latin for "small-flowered." Some Native Americans ate the bulbs of this genus.

NCEL LADUE

Brown Bells

KAREN WIESE

Davidson's Fritillary

DAVIDSON'S FRITILLARY
Fritillaria pinetorum
Lily Family (Liliaceae)

Description: Uncommon perennial rising up to 16" from a bulb. The 4–20 linear leaves occur along the stem and are reduced above. The erect, bell-shaped flowers are up to 1 ½" wide and have 3 petal-like sepals and 3 petals; each of these is purple with green mottling. The style is divided nearly to the base.

May–July

Habitat/Range: Shaded areas, especially granitic slopes, in mixed coniferous forest in the central and southern Sierra Nevada.

Comments: The species name is Latin for "dice box," referring to the shape of the fruit. The species name is Latin for "of the pine forests," referring to its habitat.

GLOSSARY

alternate. Leaf placement along a stem with leaves adjacent to but not opposite from one another (*see* illustration p. 9).

annual. A plant that completes its life cycle in one year (*compare* biennial; perennial).

ascending. Curving upward from the base.

axil. The upper angle between the stem and a leaf or branch.

banner. The uppermost and usually the largest petal of flowers in the pea family (Fabaceae) (*see* illustration p. 10).

basal. Located at or near the base of a plant.

batholith. A vast field of rock that underlies a mountain range; literally means "deep rock."

bell-shaped. Describes a flower with a corolla that widens abruptly at the base.

biennial. A plant that completes its life cycle in two growing years (*compare* annual; perennial).

bract. A small, leaf- or petal-like structure that occurs immediately below the inflorescence or along a stem.

bulb. A short, fleshy, underground stem and the leaves or leaf bases attached to and surrounding it.

calyx. Collective term for all the sepals of a flower; the outermost or lowermost whorl of flower parts, generally green and enclosing the flower in bud (*see* illustration, p. 10).

catkin. A spike of unisexual flowers; a spike of either female or male flowers.

circumboreal. Found around the world at northern latitudes.

clasping. Describes a leaf partially or wholly surrounding the stem.

cleistogamous. Describes budlike flowers that do not open and thus are self-pollinated.

compound leaf. A leaf divided into distinct parts called leaflets (*see* illustration, p. 9).

conifers. Shrubs and trees, such as firs and pines, that bear their flowers and fruits in the form of scaly cones.

corm. A short, thick, underground stem often surrounded by dry (not fleshy) leaves or leaf bases.

corolla. Collective term for all the petals of a flower; immediately inside or above the calyx (*see* illustration, p. 10).

cyme. A branched inflorescence in which the uppermost flowers open before the lower flowers (*compare* panicle; *see* illustration, p. 11).

deciduous. Plants that lose their leaves once a year, at the end of the growing season (*compare* evergreen).

disk flower. In the sunflower family (Asteraceae), the 5-lobed flowers that lack a long raylike lobe; these generally occur in the center of the flower head (*compare* ray flower; *see* illustration, p. 10).

dissected. Irregularly, sharply, and deeply cut but not compound; refers primarily to leaves.

elliptic. Having the shape of a flattened circle, with both tips evenly pointed (*see* illustration, p. 10).

endemic. Native to a well-defined geographic area and restricted to that area.

entire. With leaf margins that are continuous and smooth (*see* illustration, p. 9)

evergreen. Plants that never lack green leaves; the leaves may fall off throughout the year, but never all at once (*compare* deciduous).

exserted. Extending beyond.

filament. The anther stalk; the threadlike portion of the stamen (*see* illustration, p. 10).

flower head. A composite inflorescence of individual flowers; in the sunflower family (Asteraceae), a flower head resembles one flower but is actually many (*see* illustration, p. 10).

funnel-shaped. Describes a flower with a corolla that widens gradually from the base.

gland. A small, often round body that usually secretes a sticky substance.

glandular. Bearing glands.

hood. 1) A floral appendage in the milkweeds (Asclepiadaceae) that is attached to the filament. 2) Anything with a curved, protective shape like the hood of a jacket.

inflorescence. A flower or an entire cluster of flowers and associated structures (such as bracts and flower stalks), but not foliage leaves.

keel. The two lowermost, fused petals of flowers in the pea family (Fabaceae) (*see* illustration, p. 10).

lanceolate. A narrow shape that is widest at the base and tapered to a tip at the other end (*see* illustration, p. 10).

lateral. Referring to the sides of a structure.

leaf. Stem appendage that is generally green and composed of a stalk and a flat photosynthetic surface.

leaflet. One leaflike unit of a compound leaf.

leaf litter. The uppermost layer of decomposing leaves and microorganisms on the soil.

liniment. A soothing liquid medicine specifically formulated to be absorbed through the skin. Liniments are rubbed on the skin to target muscles and ligaments.

lobe. 1) The free tips of an otherwise fused structure, such as petals. 2) An extension or bulge, such as on the margin of a leaf or petal (*see* illustration, p. 9).

margin. Referring to the edge of something, usually a leaf.

native to California. A species that was in California prior to European contact.

nectary gland. The structure in a flower that secretes nectar, a nutritive solution that is consumed by insects and birds, which often pollinate the plant.

node. The joint of a stem where leaves, branches, or flowers arise.

nonnative. A plant that occurs as a direct or indirect consequence of human activity, such as an Old World weed, and was not here prior to European contact.

oblanceolate. Broader and rounder at the apex and tapering at the base.

oblong. A shape that is longer than wide, with nearly parallel sides and rounded corners (*see* illustration, p. 10).

obovate. A shape that is wider at the tip and tapered at the base (*see* illustration, p. 10).

opposite. Refers to leaves arranged along a stem, directly across from each other.

ovate. A shape that is wider at the base and tapered to a tip at the other end (*see* illustration, p. 10).

panicle. A branched inflorescence in which the lowermost flowers open before the upper ones (*compare* cyme; *see* illustration p. 11).

pappus. On individual flowers on the flower heads of a member of the sunflower family (Asteraceae), the whorl of scales or bristles in the place where the sepals would be expected.

partial parasite. Also called a hemiparasite, a plant that usually contains chlorophyll and may be an obligate parasite (which must have a host in order to complete its life cycle) or a facultative parasite (which can complete its life cycle without a host).

perennial. A plant that lives more than two years or growing seasons and is not woody above the ground, differentiated in this book from subshrubs (*compare* annual; biennial).

perianth. Collectively, the calyx and corolla; used in this book when they are indistinguishable.

petals. The individual parts of the corolla; often brightly colored.

pinnate. In this book, refers to the arrangement of a compound leaf having leaflets in two rows on opposite sides of the axis (*see* illustration, p. 10).

pistil. The female reproductive structure of a flower, composed of an ovary, one or more pollen-receiving stigmas at the tip, and one or more styles between the ovary and the stigma (*see* illustration, p. 10).

poultice. An herbal preparation made by mashing plant structures and a liquid (usually water) to form a wet paste.

prostrate. Lying flat on the ground.

raceme. An unbranched inflorescence of flowers on a flower stalk that open from bottom to top.

ray. A primary, radiating branch in an umbel (*see* illustration, p. 10).

ray flower. In the sunflower family (Asteraceae), a flower that bears a straplike extension on one side of the corolla. Ray flowers occur on the margin of the flower head and superficially resemble "petals" (*see* illustration, p. 10).

reflexed. Bent or curved downward or backward.

rhizome. An underground, horizontal stem.

rosette. A radiating cluster of leaves, generally at or near ground level.

saucer-shaped. Describes a flower with a corolla that is open and wide at the base.

sepals. The individual parts of the calyx; often greenish, but sometimes petal-like.

serpentine. A type of rock that yields a soil with high levels of toxic metals and low levels of necessary plant nutrients. Though most serpentine occurs in the coast range of California, there are isolated pockets of this rock in the Sierra Nevada.

serrate. Having margins with sharp teeth (*see* illustration, p. 9).

shrub. A woody, branched plant of relatively short height, less than 15' tall.

spherical. Ball- or globe-shaped; in this book, refers to flowers and inflorescence shapes.

spike. An elongate, unbranched inflorescence of stalkless flowers.

stamen. The male reproductive structure of a flower, composed of a stalklike filament with a pollen-producing anther at the tip.

staminode. Sterile stamen, having no anther.

star-shaped. Describes a flower that has petals radiating from a common point.

stigma. The top portion of a pistil on which pollen is normally deposited.

style. The stalklike portion of the pistil that connects the stigma to the ovary.

subshrub. A plant with the lower stems woody, with upper stems and twigs not woody and dying back seasonally.

succession. The predictable progression of different plant communities occupying a specific site as resources change.

tendril. A slender, often stemlike, coiling structure that is used for climbing and support.

throat. In flowers with fused petals, the inside of the flower, above the tube and below the lobes.

tincture. An extract of a plant made by soaking it in a solution, usually alcohol. A few drops of the extract is taken internally, usually added to a tea.

trumpet-shaped. Describes a flower with flared, spreading corolla lobes, abruptly tapering to the base.

tube. In flowers with fused petals, the fused portion at the base.

tuber. A short, thick, fleshy underground stem for nutrient storage and sometimes propagation.

tubular. Describes a flower shaped like a cylinder, fused at the base.

umbel. An inflorescence with three to many rays that radiate from a central point like the spokes of an umbrella.

urn-shaped. Describes a flower shaped like a spittoon.

vernal pool. An area with a seasonal pond, having a unique complement of organisms adapted to site conditions.

vine. A trailing or climbing plant.

whorl. A group of three of more structures of the same kind (such as leaves) at one node.

wing. 1) Any thin, flat extension of a surface. 2) The lateral petals of flowers in the pea family (Fabaceae) (*see* illustration, p. 10).

SELECTED REFERENCES

Bakker, Elna S. 1971. *An Island Called California: An Ecological Introduction to Its Natural Communities*. Berkeley and Los Angeles: University of California Press.

Barbour, Michael G., Bruce Pavlik, Frank Drysdale, and Susan Lindstrom. 1993. *California's Changing Landscapes*. Berkeley and Los Angeles: University of California Press.

Barbour, Michael G., and Jack Major. 1988. *Terrestrial Vegetation of California*. Sacramento: California Native Plant Society.

Blackwell, Laird, R. 1999. *Wildflowers of the Sierra Nevada and the Central Valley*. Redmond, Wash.: Lone Pine Publishing.

Carville, Julie Stauffer. 1989. *Hiking Tahoe's Wildflower Trails*. Redmond, Wash.: Lone Pine Publishing.

Chatfield, Kimball. 1997. *Medicine from the Mountains: Medicinal Plants of the Sierra Nevada*. South Lake Tahoe, Calif.: Range of Light Press.

Coleman, Ronald A. 1995. *The Wild Orchids of California*. Ithaca: Cornell University Press.

Fauver, Toni. 1991. *Wildflower Walking in the Lakes Basin of the Northern Sierra*. Orinda, Calif.: Fauver and Steinbach.

————. 1998. *Wildflower Walks and Roads of the Sierra Gold Country*. Grass Valley, Calif.: Comstock Bonanza Press.

Graf, Michael. 1999. *Plants of the Tahoe Basin*. Berkeley and Los Angeles: University of California Press.

Hickman, James C., ed. 1993. *The Jepson Manual: Higher Plants of California*. Berkeley and Los Angeles: University of California Press.

Horn, Elizabeth L. 1998. *Sierra Nevada Wildflowers*. Missoula, Mont.: Mountain Press.

Moore, Michael. 1993. *Medicinal Plants of the Pacific West*. Santa Fe, N.M.: Red Crane Books.

Muir, John. [1911] 1979. *My First Summer in the Sierra*. Reprint, Boston: Houghton Mifflin.

————. [1894] 1991. *The Mountains of California*. Reprint, Berkeley: Ten Speed Press.

————. [1914] 1988. *The Yosemite*. Reprint, San Francisco: Sierra Club Books.

Munz, Philip A. 1963. *California Mountain Wildflowers*. Berkeley and Los Angeles: University of California Press.

Munz, Philip A., and David D. Keck. 1973. *A California Flora and Supplement.* Berkeley and Los Angeles: University of California Press.

Niehaus, Theodore F. 1976. *A Field Guide to Pacific States Wildflowers.* Peterson Field Guide Series. Boston: Houghton Mifflin.

Nilsson, Karen B. 1994. *A Wild Flower by Any Other Name: Sketches of Pioneer Naturalists Who Named Our Western Plants.* Yosemite National Park, Calif.: Yosemite Association.

Ornduff, Robert. 1974. *Introduction to California Plant Life.* Berkeley and Los Angeles: University of California Press.

Parsons, Mary Elizabeth. [1907] 1966. *The Wild Flowers of California.* 3d ed. Reprint, New York: Dover Publications.

Sawyer, John O., Jr., and Todd Keeler-Wolf. 1995. *A Manual of California Vegetation.* Sacramento: California Native Plant Society.

Smith, Gladys. 1984. *A Flora of the Tahoe Basin and Neighboring Areas and Supplement.* San Francisco: University of San Francisco.

Stewart, Bob. 1997. *Common Butterflies of California.* Point Reyes Station, Calif.: West Coast Lady Press.

Storer, Tracy I., and Robert L. Usinger. 1963. *Sierra Nevada Natural History: An Illustrated Handbook.* Berkeley and Los Angeles: University of California Press.

Tilford, Gregory L., 1997. *Edible and Medicinal Plants of the West.* Missoula, Mont.: Mountain Press.

Weeden, Norman F. 1986. *A Sierra Nevada Flora.* Berkeley: Wilderness Press.

Whitney, Stephen. 1979. *A Sierra Club Naturalist's Guide to the Sierra Nevada.* San Francisco: Sierra Club Books.

Zwinger, Ann H., and Beatrice E. Willard. 1986. *Land above the Trees: A Guide to American Alpine Tundra.* New York: Harper and Row.

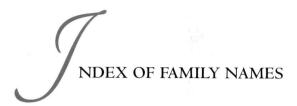

INDEX OF FAMILY NAMES

INDEX OF PLANT NAMES

About the Author

Karen Wiese works as a plant ecologist in mine reclamation for the California Department of Conservation. Karen has a master of science degree from the University of California at Davis in Plant Protection and Pest Management and a bachelor of science degree in Natural Resources from Michigan State University. Karen has been guiding natural history hikes throughout the West for over a decade and has a business organizing and leading natural history hiking and backpacking trips for all ages. Karen is active in the California Native Plant Society and an avid hiker and backpacker. Karen owns an organic farm in the foothills of the Sierra Nevada, where she gardens year round with her three cats.

Karen Wiese

About Some of the Photographers

The native plants and seasonal landscapes of the northern Sierra Nevada inspire the work of professional photographer Karen Callahan. Her photographs are featured in publications as well as botanical note cards and prints. She is President of the Redbud Chapter of the California Native Plant Society and a volunteer for Tahoe National Forest's Sensitive Plant Program.

Richard Hanes, a retired US Forest Service soil scientist, has been photographing plants, particularly sensitive species, for more than 30 years. Richard is the Rare Plant Coordinator for the Redbud Chapter of the California Native Plant Society and a volunteer for Tahoe National Forest's Sensitive Plant Program.